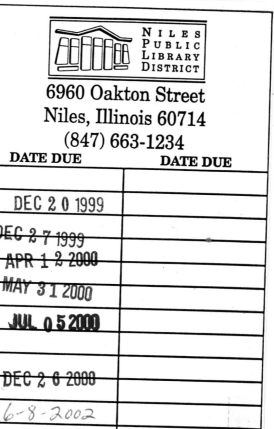

The Wiccan Book of Ceremonies and Rituals

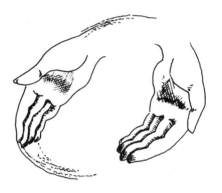

Patricia Telesco

A Citadel Press Book
Published by Carol Publishing Group

A Citadel Press Book
Published by Carol Publishing Group
Citadel Press is a registered trademark of Carol Communications, Inc.

Editorial, sales and distribution, rights and permissions inquiries should be addressed to Carol Publishing Group, 120 Enterprise Avenue, Secaucus, N.J. 07094.

In Canada: Canadian Manda Group, One Atlantic Avenue, Suite 105, Toronto, Ontario M6K 3E7

Carol Publishing Group books may be purchased in bulk at special discounts for sales promotion, fund-raising, or educational purposes. Special editions can be created to specifications. For details, contact Special Sales Department, Carol Publishing Group, 120 Enterprise Avenue, Secaucus, N.J. 07094.

Manufactured in the United States of America

10 9 8 7 6 5 4 3 2 1

Library of Congress Cataloging-in-Publication Data

Telesco, Patricia, 1960–
    The Wiccan book of ceremonies and rituals / Patricia Telesco.
        p.   cm.
    ISBN 0–8065–2031–0 (pbk.)
    1. Witchcraft   2. Ritual.   3. Rites and ceremonies.   I. Title.
BF1566.T35   1998
133.4'3—dc21   98–28382
                                                      CIP

*Let your holidays be associated
with great public events,
and they may be the life of patriotism
as well as a source of relaxation
and personal employment*

—Tyron Edwards

Contents

Introduction

'Tis but the same rehearsal of the past, and History with all her volumes vast, hath but one page.

—Lord Byron

Ceremonies and rituals are an integral part of the human experience. Throughout history, ritualistic festivals and observances have become an amazing repository for custom and tradition. In reviewing the world's celebrations, it is also evident that each ceremony intimately depicts the culture, history, and beliefs of the participants.

While ceremonies vary from country to country, civilization to civilization, and religion to religion, their essential soul remains the same. They have a unifying spirit that draws people together to honor communal bonds. Ritual, in any setting, becomes a medium for the outward expression of this spirit.

Each ritual performed provided our ancestors with an annual rhythm that encouraged coherence in communities. Just as important, each cadence included guidance on when to sow crops, times to sing of the honored dead, moments to welcome life—just generally commemorate everything it means to be human. Wiccans are no exception to this metered framework. In fact, many symbols, songs, and activities in modern ceremonies have roots partially in the Wiccan/Pagan tradition and in the Wheel of the year. Traditionally this figurative Wheel has eight festival-spokes that take place an average of forty-five days apart.

Festival-spokes mark another juncture in the sun's annual journey through the sky, and commemorate the metaphorical value of this timing. During Candlemas (December 2), for example, people light candles to symbolically give strength to the sun so it might begin overcoming the last vestiges of winter. On a deeper spiritual level, this represents banishing our personal shadows with the light of truth and virtue.

Other Wiccan festivals were designed to revere the gods and goddesses of a specific pantheon. Exactly which pantheon, of course, depends on the magical tradition. Returning to our illustration, in some areas Candlemas is also called Brigid's Day. In the Irish tradition, Brigid was a goddess who nurtured the woodlands and forests, as well as being a protectress of poets. So this festival often invokes her power with libations of ale, tree plantings, and animal blessings.

The remaining celebrations of the Wiccan tradition strive to meet intimate human needs by remembering the important events that shape both individuals and whole civilizations. One illustration here is the Rite of Passage, in which children who have come of age are welcomed as adults in the magical community. This ritual acknowledges the growth of the child by giving him or her new responsibilities at home and in the circle, and even sometimes a new magical name to use in the latter setting.

With this background in mind, the purpose of this book is threefold. First, in part 1, you will learn the mechanics of Wiccan ritual, including its basic organization and commonly used tools. This part also explains that "rituals" are something you already perform, knowingly or unknowingly. The information in this section acts as a blueprint, allowing you to personalize and perform any Wiccan rituals in the future.

Part 2 reviews the Wiccan Wheel. Wiccans recognize that

Earth is a valuable resource; it nurtures the questing spirit on its road to enlightenment. So we observe festivals that help bring us closer to nature's rhythms, and make us more aware of her lessons, including those of the Sun, the moon, and seasons.

Commemorating the Wiccan Wheel also encourages taking time out of our hectic schedules for communing regularly with the Sacred Powers. In a world whose black-and-white boundaries are so often lost to gray uncertainty, this time is very important to personal and spiritual development. Whatever your vision of the Divine, these rituals reconnect you with that Source as something that can manifest powerfully in your daily life.

Finally, part 4 speaks to the human element—the moments in life that should be honored and remembered in a special fashion, but that often get glossed over in our warp-speed society. This section provides guidance on how to integrate your special experiences through personalized ritual. It goes on to share a few examples of rites that people have created for just this purpose.

As you will see throughout these pages, Wicca is a creative and diversified faith. Consequently, my portrait of Wiccan ritual is but one illustration of how it can be done. Other practitioners may have vastly different approaches. This variety is part of what makes Wicca wonderful. Our philosophy advocates and stimulates personal vision as an integral part of the spiritual experience.

Adapting and employing Wiccan ritual can be a very satisfying experience. It encourages us to celebrate every moment of living as something truly special. It reminds us that spirituality is not something separate from our daily reality. Finally, and most important, rituals allow our lives to become an act of worship, expressing the Sacred that abides within us, and all things.

PART I

Ritual in Review

By these festival rites from the age that is past,
to the age that is waiting before.

—Samuel Gilman

Wicca is a sacred belief system based in Nature and Goddess worship, bearing many similarities to Native American traditions. In Wicca, a practitioner honors the sacredness of all things by approaching life in an Earth-friendly, spiritually centered way. This boils down to maintaining an intimate awareness of personal responsibility, treating other religions with tolerance and respect, venerating the Divine, and living in reciprocity with Nature. By so doing, a practitioner's every thought and action can potentially express the positive, empowering energy called magic. The idea here is to *become* the magic in which we believe, not simply wield it.

But what exactly is this "magic"? Defining the term is difficult, due in part to hundreds of years of misunderstanding. Effectively, magical power equates to the energy of life that exists in all things, including you. Think of this energy as strands of light that the magical practitioner gathers into a potent bundle through the use of charms, spells, and rituals. Once the fibers are assembled, they can then be woven together into a functional thought-form for specific goals.

This process is not without some limits, specifically those set by morality, universal law, and common sense. Wicca means "Craft of the Wise," the hope being that we learn to use this potent tool with sagacity, sensitivity, and insight. To accomplish this, however, we each must recognize our divine nature. Harder still, we must recognize and trust in the inherent metaphysical potential this nature offers. The tinder of magic lies within your heart and soul just waiting to be ignited. Ritual is one way of bringing those embers to life, and keeping them burning as part of your everyday reality.

1

What Is Ritual?

Humans are highly ritualistic by nature. We tend to use the same coffee cup each day, drive to work by the same route, arrange the silverware the same way in the drawer each time the dishes get done, and so forth. These actions constitute mini rituals that we follow daily, giving our lives form, coherence, and an air of comfortable familiarity. Yet the idea of personally enacting a more formalized ritual evokes unsettled feelings deep within some individuals.

This is because most people are unaccustomed to the concept that you can become your own priest or priestess. In truth, however, you already execute this role every day in the decision-making process—when you choose between various options, between "good" and "bad," between action and inaction. By so doing, the reins of fate remain firmly in hand and you become the guiding force that is normally equated with spiritual leadership.

Taking this concept one step further, all of us have the capacity to fulfill a spiritual calling in our lives. All that remains is to give it a try, and trust in our capacity to do so! This chapter will provide fundamental information on how rituals are constructed, what tools are used, and how to prepare for the rite.

More important, this chapter explains the "whys" of ritual

configurations, implements, and the preparation process. Enacting any ceremony without this understanding turns the entire procedure into a rote pantomime—without feeling, without personal meaning, and without power. Consequently, I encourage trusting your instincts and vision for the right way to handle any ritual setting. The suggestions in this book are like the black and white outlines of a coloring book. Apply to them your soulful crayons, and creatively bring the ritual's portrait to life.

Also, please know that these guidelines are only generalities. Ritual ranks among the primary techniques used in Wicca to gather power; it is applied for personal worship, spiritual growth, and as a way of meeting common needs. Yet every Wiccan tradition has unique characteristics, meaning rituals vary from group to group. What's provided here is a "generic" construct to which you can add your personal path and insight for the most meaningful and successful results.

Remember, rituals do not have to be fancy, formal, or exactingly precise to be powerful and transformational. The Sacred Powers care more about your motivations, and the feeling you put into the rite, than they do about the trappings. So try not to get overly self-conscious.

Ambience

Step one for enacting successful rituals is having a suitable environment in which to work. Just as most people would not randomly run through a church, the area prepared for ritual needs to have an ambience that inspires a respectful attitude in the attendees. Before this puts you off, however, rest assured that this doesn't require redecorating your home to look like a cathedral! Instead, it means thinking ahead and doing some practical planning. For example, to ensure that your ritual doesn't get interrupted, turn off your phone, ask the participants (if any) to arrive on time, and ask family and friends not to drop in. Almost everyone understands the need for a little privacy, so don't be shy about asking for some.

Next, consider the ritual room itself. Is it straightened up so that clutter doesn't interfere with your focus? Move whatever furniture is necessary to make room for the participants. Also, make sure that whatever activities you have planned can take place safely. Keep candles well away from curtains, for example, and sharp implements such as ritual daggers far out of the reach of household pets or children.

If possible, consider holding rituals outdoors. A great writer once said that the groves were gods' first temples; they can remain so if you're fortunate enough to have a field nearby. Such a setting will add a lovely energy to any ritual.

Just as with your home, however, look around the space and take care of any stones, sticks, or holes that could trip you or others. This type of prep work all sounds rather bland, but applying the rule of "safety first" from the outset makes for much more enjoyable rituals in the long run.

Besides the setting, several other touches can help create an effective ritual ambience. These include aromatics, decorations, and music. Beginning with aromatics, many Wiccans smudge the ritual area using cedar and sage incense. Smudging basically entails moving the smoke through the room with your hand, with a feather, or by moving the brazier. The cedar and sage help clear the air of random energies.

Add other thematic incense before and during the ritual. For example, a Handfasting (similar to a wedding) might include rose incense, rose being the flower of love. For those with a sensitivity to incense, try gatherings of flowers or potpourri instead. These come in just as many varieties as incense, and you won't spend the whole ritual sneezing! To illustrate, the space in which the Handfasting is held could be encircled by rose petals, or by any other herbs and blossoms associated with love—lemon verbena, daisy, lavender, mint.

The additional benefit of flowers is that they become part of the decorations that accent your ritual's theme, and sometimes are part of associated spells. Throughout the ritual portion of this book decorating ideas are suggested, but please feel free to get creative. The power and personal satisfaction that you gain from any ritual directly relate to how much you think about what it means to you, and express that meaning in the sacred space. Decorations serve other functions besides just looking good. Sometimes they become part of the ritual itself. For example, during the Handfasting participants might loosely tie ribbons in a nearby tree and make wishes for the man and woman. The knot of the ribbon "holds" the magic until the wind releases the wishes.

Suitable decorations to consider for any occasion include thematically shaped or colored candles, tablecloths, paintings, photographs, balloons, crystals, torches, and so forth. For more ideas, take a walk through any party supply store. And while you're at it, don't forget to decorate yourself. Wear a chaplet of flowers, don special garb, and put on personally meaningful jewelry for the event. The old saying "clothes make the man" has significance here. Wearing special clothing for ritual, and keeping it separate from normal apparel, changes your focus toward the esoteric; this puts you in the right frame of mind to begin (see also "Personal Touches" on page 17).

Finally, think about music. Thanks to the wonders of technology, portable tape and CD players are easy to come by these days, as is a diversity of New Age music. Obviously, exactly what music you choose depends largely on the ritual and its participants. In a Handfasting, the couple may want a popular contemporary song playing in the background. Other rituals will be different.

Just because this is a magical setting, doesn't mean that you can't look at all music as having magical potential. To know how to best use music to set the ambience, think about how it makes you feel. What mental images does the music engender? For example, Kenny Loggins's "Return to Pooh Corner" is perfect for a child's naming ceremony or the first part of a Rite of Passage, because of the imagery it presents.

All in all, creating the perfect space for your ritual takes nothing more than a little forethought and ingenuity. But remember that though there will be moments when life doesn't allow such planning, all is not lost. Our needs don't always have good timing! Go ahead and enact the ritual just as you are, where you are. The trappings of a ritual are only helpmates for humans who sometimes feel awkward about working with sacred energies. In and of themselves, the accoutrements do nothing. You give them meaning and activate their potential in the sacred space. Your spiritual nature—not your tools—gives birth to the magic.

Always remember that life itself is a ritual, and an act of worship. Anything else becomes icing on the cake.

Personal Preparation

Once you've created a suitable atmosphere, the next step is preparing yourself. You are about to become your own priest or priestess, and the vehicle for sacred energies. For this process to work effectively and have positive results, you need to be ready physically, mentally, and spiritually.

For the physical dimension, I recommend being healthy and well rested. When you are sick or tired, the physical negatives can translate into spiritually discordant energy that can misdirect your magic. Additionally, consider taking an herbal bath or shower before starting, to symbolically wash away any tensions, anger, and other bits of stress that we all tend to carry.

Besides this, try dabbing some personally significant herbal oil on the chakras located at the top of your head (crown), forehead (the Third Eye), and heart. These three are the most active during rituals. Apply the oil by swirling it clockwise to symbolically open the energy center. Some choices of oils include:

For peace Lavender, pennyroyal, or violet
For power Carnation, ginger, or cinnamon
For psychism Jasmine, marigold, or thyme
For purification Cedar, coconut, or lemon

During the anointing process, you can add a supplication to the Sacred Powers if you feel so inclined. Here is one example: *"Let my mind be open to understanding (Crown), let my spirit be open to insight (Third Eye), let my heart be open to truth* (heart)." Performing the supplication accomplishes two things: it helps you focus on and access your inner spiritual nature as well as welcoming the Divine as a copilot in the ritual process.

For mental preparation, meditation and visualization work well. To meditate means to think deeply, in this case specifically about the ritual and what it means to you. Consider your motivations during this time, and make sure that your heart is in the right place. If you're angry or otherwise ill disposed, it's best to put off the ritual until your emotions are more balanced.

Begin meditating using breath as a focus. Sit comfortably, close your eyes, and listen to your breathing. Take deep, even breaths— in through your nose, out through your mouth. Try to keep these connected in a never-ending circle.

After establishing this pattern, listen to your heartbeat. It is the rhythm of life, and the cadence of your spirit. Let it guide the pace of your breathing cycles. As you do this, begin to imagine a brilliant, sparkling white light pouring down like a waterfall from overhead. The light-energy fills each breath you take, removing any doubts, fears, and tensions when exhaled. When all the negativity abates, the light saturates your being with positive power to take into the ritual space.

Finally, at this point a brief prayer to the Sacred Powers can help align your spiritual nature. Think of this step as a way of hooking up an interdimensional telephone line to establish rapport between yourself and whatever image of the Divine you follow. This figurative conference call makes it easier to maintain or reestablish contact in the ritual space. Here is one example:

Great God and Goddess, Master and Mistress of all Creation,
I ask you to make me an instrument of light and truth.

Let my spirit and heart be loving and insightful
in the working of magic.
Guide my efforts and energy that they harm none.
So mote it be.

If you follow a specific divine visage or work with a cultural pantheon, you may wish to substitute the name(s) of that Being in prayers like this. Once contacted, this Spirit, this Divinity, binds the elements of your circle into a cooperative force that helps direct your magic (also see "Sacred Space" on page 22).

The Altar and Magical Tools

The word *altar* comes from a Latin term meaning "high place," indicating its connection with the Divine. Ancient people used the altar for enacting sacrifices. This is also where offerings to the gods were left, including food, beverages, incense, and gems. Later, it became a place of worship.

The intimation of an altar as a place of veneration remains in Wicca, which is why being prepared is so important. Just as with our ancestors, this is where you will invoke the Powers for help in your magic. This is also where your ritual tools are placed until you need them (see the list below).

The implements of Wicca bear similarities to those used in many other belief systems. Unlike other religious people, however, not all Wiccans use the same tools. This happens for several reasons. First, ritual implements vary significantly depending on a rite's construct. Second, different cultural expressions of Wicca suggest the use of different tools. Third, Wiccans strongly rely on personalization as a key to spiritual growth and enlightenment, and they choose tools that reflect this individuality.

Finally, Wiccans believe that tools are simply that—helpmates. They assist with magic in much the way hammers help carpenters. Even without hammers, of course, carpenters know their art. So, too, the Wiccan knows that magic comes from within, not from any one tool. Nonetheless, tools do make things easier. They give your conscious mind something concrete upon which to fix its attention, freeing up your intuitive nature.

When you begin to look for your magical implements, I recommend choosing tools that appeal to both your senses (visual, tactile, and so forth) and your pocketbook. The usefulness of these objects is determined by their meaning to you, and how you employ them, not the price tag. Just be certain to cleanse and charge all tools before putting them on the altar, to ensure that no random energies hinder your magic. To accomplish this, pass the tool through cleansing smoke (such as cedar, pine, or myrrh), then leave it in the light of the sun and a waning moon for three hours each (the number of body, mind, and spirit). If circumstances don't allow for either, meditate with the implement; visualize it being filled with the same brilliant light that you used to prepare yourself for ritual.

The following list includes tools that Wiccans of various traditions are known to use, and notes each item's symbolic value(s):

Aspurger This may be a branch of heather or any other item that can sprinkle purifying water around the circle. You may also choose other fresh plant snippets or tree branches that symbolically match the purpose of the ritual. The nice part about this approach is that the fresh greenery has a decorative appeal, too.

Athame A two-edged knife or sword that represents the masculine half of the universe, the two-edged nature of power, and the delicate balance we must maintain to wield magic for the greatest good. The point on the athame helps direct power from the practitioner outward toward its goal. Some Wiccans use their athames to harvest the magical herbs they use in rituals, while others keep this blade set apart solely for use in the sacred space. Look for knives or swords at antiques shops, flea markets, and cutlery stores.

Brazier This is a type of incense burner attached to a chain; it can be used to aspurge the sacred space with cleansing smoke easily and safely. These can sometimes be acquired at religious supply stores.

Candles Candles represent the Fire element as well as the ever-burning flames of the Spirit within the human heart. Depending on their color, candles sometime symbolize other elements or the goal of the ritual, too. For example, a blue candle could be placed on the western side of the altar to depict the element Water, or it could embody the energy of peace in a Forgiveness Ritual (see also "Personal Touches").

Cauldron Cauldrons symbolize the Water element. They also act as a Goddess emblem, bearing both a womblike shape and three legs, which represent the triune Maiden, Mother, and Crone as the counterparts to the Son, Father, and Grandfather. Check Asian gift shops and New Age stores to find these in various sizes and materials.

Crystals and Minerals Depending on their shapes and colors, stones may represent the elements, the God and Goddess, or the nature of the ritual; they may also simply be placed on the altar to amplify energy. Clear quartz is particularly suited to the latter application. Examples of some common stones and their correspondences include:

Stone	Element	God/Goddess	Type of Magic
Red agate	Fire	God	Courage, safety
Amethyst	Water	Goddess	Spirituality, psychism
Aventurine	Air	God	Conscious mind, money
Brass	Fire	God	Banishing, cleansing
Cat's eye	Earth	Goddess	Insight, abundance
Coral	Water	Goddess	Health, peace
Green jasper	Earth	Goddess	Sleep, emotions
Quartz, point	Fire	God	Power, protection
Quartz, tumbled	Water	Goddess	Prophesy, healing
Tin	Air	God	Fortune telling, luck

The least-expensive sources for crystals include science hobby stores, geologists, and rock and mineral shows. For more ideas on how to use crystals, metals, and minerals effectively in ritual, I suggest consulting *Crystal, Gem and Mineral Magic* by Scott Cunningham (Llewellyn Publications, 1995).

Cup The cup is another feminine, Water symbol that holds beverages. The beverages may be consumed during a ritual as a way of uniting the participants or internalizing energy. Some may also be poured on the ground as a libation to Earth and the gods. Watch for unique cups at secondhand shops or garage sales.

Feather or Fan Symbols of the Air element, feathers and hand fans, are sometimes used to move incense around the sacred space, dispersing any negative energy. If you use a feather you're found outside, make sure to clean it off with warm water to prevent disease.

God and Goddess Figures Many objects function as god and goddess emblems, including carvings, portraits, and statues of those from specific pantheons. You can also represent the Goddess with any round or oval object, and the God with any square or oblong object. One source for various-sized figurines is lawn and garden shops. The statuary sold at these outlets is very durable, and withstands a lot of minor accidents without getting damaged. If possible, find those that best reflect your vision of the Divine.

Incense A representation of both the Air and Fire elements, incense is usually chosen for its magical attributes so that it improves the vibrations in the ritual space. Here is a sample list of aromas and their magical characteristics:

Scent	*Attributes*
Apple	Health, love
Banana	Abundance, fertility
Cedar	Prosperity, cleansing
Frankincense	Banishing, warding, purification
Heather	Luck, weather magic

Jasmine	Prophesy, relationships
Lavender	Peace, rest, joy
Mint	Safe travel, passion, health
Orange	Devotion, good fortune
Rose	Love, foresight
Sage	Cleansing, wisdom
Vanilla	Passion, conscious mind

Incense and potpourri are readily available even in supermarkets these days. You can also make your own incense by combining small pieces of a very dry aromatic wood (such as sandalwood) with powdered pantry spices. This type of incense requires a fire source (self-burning charcoal, for instance) to burn, but has the advantage of already bearing your personal energy. Again, make sure to choose the herbs according to your goals. For the most pleasing results, don't use more than three ingredients.

For more ideas on using herbs effectively in any magical procedure, consult *Cunningham's Encyclopedia of Magical Herbs* (Scott Cunningham, Llewellyn Publications, 1988) or *The Herbal Arts* (Patricia Telesco, Citadel, 1998).

Pentagram For Wiccans, the pentagram functions more as a symbol of faith than as a tool. Pentagrams are sometimes painted or embroidered onto the altar cloth. Alternatively, they appear as stained-glass decorations, on the chalice, and in ritual jewelry. The five points of the pentagram represent four or five elements, depending on your viewpoint. Earth, Air, Fire, and Water constitute four elements; the fifth is sometimes referred to as Ether, or it can represent the practitioner. Finally, the center of the pentagram is where elemental powers meet, mingle, and work together, making the spark of magic.

Smudge stick A bundle of herbs, often cedar and sage, burned and used to purify the sacred space of any lingering negative energies. It is a good alternative to a brazier, but for safety purposes you should have a small bowl of water nearby with which to douse the burning herbs. Buy smudge sticks at Native American or New

Age outlets, or make one yourself from fresh sage: cut long (six- to eight-inch) strands of dried sage and bind them tightly together at one end. Next, crisscross thread down the entire body of the bundle, tying a knot at each cross section to keep the gathering very dense. Hang this on a wall between uses to keep it dry.

Salt A good symbol of the Earth element, a handy cleansing mineral, and a protective substance. Some people sprinkle salt around the perimeter of a magic circle to help purify the area and keep any malintentioned entities firmly at bay (see also "Sacred Space"). Wiccans also use sea salt mingled in water to purify tools, sacred images, crystals, and so on.

Wand An alternative to the athame whose base material can make it a substitute for different elements as well. A wooden wand can represent Earth, while a copper one is magically aligned with Water. Just as a pointer directs your attention to a specific place, the wand directs energy, especially in casting and releasing the magic circle (see "Sacred Space").

Generally, I recommend that you make your own wand out of a fallen tree branch. Place crystals in the knots of the branch to bind their energies into the wood, choosing each stone for its magical attributes. At the tip of the branch, attach a crystal point to direct the power.

Most Wiccan traditions recommend placing the surface of the altar, such as a table or trunk, in the eastern portion of a room. This positioning has symbolic value, east being the direction of the rising sun and new beginnings, but it is *not* a **necessity**. Place your altar wherever sensibility, space, and safety allow.

The traditional base materials for altars were wood and stone. Finding a wooden surface is easiest indoors; stone surfaces work well outside. Again, this is not essential, but I don't advise using plastic or aluminum surfaces for an altar. They are not overly sturdy, and the artificial materials are magically "dead."

Realistically, any flat surface can become an altar. I know people who use everything from windowsills to the back of the toilet for this purpose. Many practitioners live cooperatively with others or in small spaces, so finding creative altar tops may be a necessity. The exact setup of your altar depends largely on what tools you decide are most important for the ritual at hand, and the space available. When you lay out the items, practicality should take precedence over visual appeal. If you're wearing long-sleeved ritual robes, for example, you don't want to be reaching across candles to get a specific implement. You also don't want so many objects on the altar that it becomes cluttered, which can metaphorically "clutter" the magical energies of the items.

Overall, let your instincts and common sense guide you. From a sensible standpoint, put the tools out so that the first one you'll need is readily available, and place matches near the candles or incense. Close your eyes for a moment, holding a tool in hand, and "feel" where its energy needs to go. This takes a little practice, but in time you will know, deep within, when an altar's energy is correctly balanced and ready for use.

Once an altar is set up, you can either leave this as a permanent part of your sacred space, or disassemble it until the next ritual. If it's a permanent fixture, keep any potentially dangerous items up high enough to discourage pets and children. I use the top of a tall bookshelf, for example. If it's a temporary assembly, consider wrapping your tools in soft white cloth (the color of protection and purity) and storing them safely away from curious hands.

Should you decide on keeping your altar as a permanent fixture, care for the area as you would a beautiful garden. Tend it lovingly, keeping it free of dust and debris. Add accents throughout the year that highlight the season, and your personal needs and goals. Enjoy this region as a visual reminder that the Sacred abides within and around you always.

Personal Touches

The rituals in parts 2, 3, and 4 are observances that people around the country have used successfully. In reading these you may find parts that you don't understand, words with which you're uncomfortable, or symbols that seem out of place in your vision and tradition. Personalization fixes these problems.

As long as you maintain congruity with the original purpose of the ritual, I encourage you to adapt these materials and make notes of your changes before you enter the sacred space. Such modifications fulfill two related purposes: they provide you with an opportunity to think seriously about what this observance means to you, and in so doing they make the entire process more meaningful and potent.

Numerous avenues exist for tweaking rituals to suit your circumstances and ideology. These include:

Alternative Timing

Magic doesn't have to come to a halt because you're scheduled to work or have the flu on a festival day. Wiccans believe that magic works outside the stricture of time, both backward and forward. Therefore, you can realistically enact a ritual anytime and anywhere; it will be just as effective. The only trick is convincing yourself of this truth!

As with your other tools, you can add in this dimension or delete it, as necessity and creativity dictate. Say, for example, that you can't celebrate Hallows. Look to the world's holidays for an alternative Festival of the Dead or New Year's Celebration—the central themes of Hallows. For more ideas on how to reconfigure your personal Wheel of the Year, read *Seasons of the Sun* (Patricia Telesco, Samuel Weiser, 1996).

As another illustration, if you can't hold a Birthday Ritual on the exact date of someone's birthday, try holding it during a full moon instead. The full moon represents things coming to fruition and maturity, so the timing of your ritual will mirror its intended theme. Look over a good astrological calendar for dates and times that could suit such situations.

Color Highlights

Psychologists have proven that color affects human moods and demeanor. By adding specific colors into the ritual space, you can help personalize and amplify the effects of an observance. Say, for example, that you want to add a healing element into a Summer's Fire Festival. This goal could be demonstrated to the Powers by covering the altar with a blue (mental tranquillity) or green (physical health) cloth.

Colors can also act as marker points for the magic circle (see "The Altar and Magical Tools," page 11, and "Sacred Space," page 22), a means of amplifying the ritual's characteristics (see "Costumes," below), and a visually appealing accent (see "Ambience," page 6). Here is an abbreviated list of colors and their metaphysical correspondences:

Red Vitality, power, purification, Fire, passion, south
Orange Friendship, warmth, the harvest
Yellow Creativity, Air, knowledge, insight, east
Green Growth, beginnings, hope, health, Earth or Water
Blue Peace, calm, insight, well-being, Water
Purple Spirituality, psychism, leadership
Brown Grounding, foundations, Earth
White Protection, safety, cleansing, the Spirit

Costumes

In ancient times numerous cultural groups used costumes and masks as integral parts of rituals. These costumes usually represented the Spirit to whom the worshipers planned to appeal for aid. If petitioning the Jaguar Spirit for health, for example, they might wear black costumes and a catlike mask. The worshipers felt the gods would be pleased by the mimicry. More important, though, the costume helped release the human spirit to commune with these powers by its visual impact on a ritual's participants.

In modern times, this type of mimicry has somewhat gone by the wayside. However, remnants from this animistic past are visible in our ritual robes and other fanciful garb. When attending a circle, people wear specially chosen outfits that represent both the occasion and the practitioner's magical outlooks. For example, someone who enjoys Greek magical traditions might don toga-style dress. Other people embroider special cultural or magical emblems on their garb, and still others prefer to perform magic without any clothing. Each approach is perfectly correct, as long as the choice of apparel matches the occasion and the magic's purpose.

Costumes inspire us to have a little fun. Choose an ensemble that puts you in the right mood and awakens your inner child who trusts wholly in miracles. In spring, consider constructing an outfit out of leaves and flowers. In winter, go to festivals in white, glitter-laden robes that look like snow on a winter's night. The possibilities are endless.

Adding Unique Activities

The construct of a ritual is only that. Anything you add gives greater definition to the magic created. For example, my mother always used to take me out stargazing when spring finally arrived. Spring just wasn't officially "here" for me until these outings started. So now I make this activity a part of my annual Spring Observance, along with a few well-placed wishes! In a group setting this might equate to telling myths about the constellations, and discussing the lessons these ancient tales impart.

This illustration highlights the importance of personal experience in any magic you undertake. What's symbolic for one person may hold little meaning for someone else. Adding activities from your childhood, family traditions, or culture can keep some wonderful memories alive.

Substituting Spells, Invocations, or Prayers

It is not as difficult as you might think to find or design customized materials for your rituals. Numerous Wiccan books on the market include spells, for instance, for almost every common need. One good tome to explore is *Spinning Spells, Weaving Wonders* (Patricia Telesco, Crossing Press, 1996). This book provides not only enchantments but also directions for creating your own spells—which can personalize rituals dramatically. You will also find some sample spells for each ritual presented.

A good example of an invocation is shown in the following section, "Sacred Space." Invocations call upon the powers of creation and the Divine to protect and aid your magic. As with spells, you can find alternative invocations in books that include rituals in their text. Try *Victorian Grimoire* (Llewellyn Publications, 1992), *The Spiral Dance* (Starhawk, Harper & Row, 1987), and *The Gaia Tradition* (Llewellyn, 1991) for samples.

You can write your own invocations using poetry (to aid memorization), free-flow writing, or spur-of-the-moment inspired speaking. When you're designing one, make sure the invocation energizes, welcomes, and honors the four elements and Spirit into your circle, Traditionally, invocations begin in the east, but I see no reason why you can't begin at alternative compass points for symbolic value (such as the south for a Fire Festival).

Finally, prayers are but a way for you to speak to the Divine in a way that's comfortable for you. Generally, the best spots to add in a prayer are right after sacred space is cast, after a special activity (using the prayer to internalize that activity), or just before the dismissal of the circle. I believe there is no "wrong" way to pray. My only suggestion is that you direct your words simply and sincerely so you can enjoy the rapport; don't worry about fancy words.

Sacred Space

*We define a new space and a new time whenever we
cast a circle to begin a ritual. The circle exists on the
boundaries of ordinary space and time; it is between the
worlds of the seen and unseen, of flashlight and starlight
consciousness, a space in which all realities meet....*
—Starhawk, *The Spiral Dance*

In Wicca, rituals start with the creation of sacred space. This
procedure marks the line between world and not world, between
your mundane life and your distinctly spiritual efforts. Within this
region you create magic, express your desire for spiritual growth,
honor Earth, and rejoice in the awareness of the Sacred within.

Once in place, sacred space establishes a protective boundary
over which devas, spirits, fairies, and other spiritual beings may
not pass without permission. Whenever magic begins, such
beings may take an active interest in the proceedings. Because not
all such creatures have human interests at heart, the protective
nature of the magic circle allows you to discern what external
energies (if any) you will welcome as a partner in the magic.

Start by standing in the center of the area you've chosen, near
the altar. From this vantage point, eye out the rough points of a
four-quartered circle so you know where each point lies. Envision
the white light of protection pouring down into you (if you're
outdoors, use the silvery white light of the moon). Begin walking
clockwise around that circle, starting in the east and carrying a
burning piece of incense.

While you walk, imagine sparkling light pouring out from you,
creating a shimmering circular boundary. If it helps, use your
wand or athame, pointing it where you want the energy to go.
Also visualize light permeating the incense smoke so that it
purifies the vibrations throughout the area.

After a complete circuit, it is time to call the quarters. This step invokes the powers of the four elements from the four corners of creation. In Wicca, each element has specific attributes, powers, and ruling entities that can aid and protect your magical efforts. Again, unless this ritual is for banishing something, the calling of the quarters begins in the east and moves clockwise, following the sun's example. Conversely, banishing rituals move counterclockwise to disperse negativity.

The chapters that follow provide specific quarter invocations that befit each celebration; below is an all-purpose invocation that you can use or adapt at any time. I suggest memorizing invocations, so that you can concentrate on the words' meaning and directing the energy, instead of the reading process.

As you repeat the invocation, move along the circle's circumference to the applicable directional point, face outward, and speak to the elemental power that resides there. If you're working in a group, simply change the "I" in each part to "we." Recite the final part of the invocation in the center of the circle to bind these powers into a cooperative force.

Calling the Quarters

EAST (Air)
Beings of Air, Breath of Creation, I welcome you. Come, protect this sacred space. May your presence give flight to the magic created, and direct it safely to fulfilling its purpose.

After saying this, light a white or yellow candle here, or place a feather, fan, or burning incense in this region to symbolize the active presence of the Air element.

SOUTH (Fire)
Beings of Fire, Flames of Cleansing, I welcome you. Come, protect this sacred space. May your presence empower the magic created, and activate it for fulfilling its purpose.

After saying this, light a red or orange candle here, place a brazier or pack of matches in this region, or turn on a nearby light to symbolize the active presence of the Fire element.

WEST (Water)

Beings of Water, Waves of Insight, I welcome you. Come, protect this sacred space. May your presence fill the magic with love, and allow it to flow freely in fulfilling its purpose.

After saying this, light a blue or purple candle here, or place a seashell, cup of water, or pinch of sand in this region to symbolize the active presence of the Water element.

NORTH (Earth)

Beings of Earth, Soil of Nurturing, I welcome you. Come, protect this sacred space. May your presence give foundations to the magic created, so it grows to maturity, fulfilling its purpose.

After saying this, light a brown or green candle here, or place a flower, rock, or pinch of soil in this region to symbolize the active presence of the Earth element.

CENTER (Spirit)

Great Spirit, Old Ones, I welcome you. Come, protect this sacred space. May your presence bind the magic created, and guide it in perfect trust to fulfill its goal. So mote it be.

After saying this, light a white candle on the center of your altar, or place there any object that you feel represents the active presence of the Spirit in the sacred space.

After invoking the quarters, the main part of the ritual ensues. Most rituals, as you will see throughout this book, include activities that highlight the purpose of the gathering and build energy. Dancing, drumming, songs, and numerous other actions can all be used to focus a ritual and the power it creates. Your choice of methods depends on the ritual itself and the desires of the participants. Once the energy reaches a pinnacle, it is directed outward toward the goal and released—otherwise it can do no good. Examples of how to accomplish this are provided with each ritual in parts 2, 3, and 4.

Closing the Circle and Grounding

When participants complete a ritual, the protected sphere created beforehand still remains. So disassembling this energy is part of the closing of any observance. To accomplish this task, begin in the west and move counterclockwise to each compass point of the circle. At each point, recite a closing such as the one below, and either blow out the candle or remove the symbolic token placed there.

Guardians and Guides All, I thank you for your presence and help. Pray, take your leave now, carrying the magic to its mark, and blessing all in your path.

Don't forget to likewise close the center point of the circle where the Spirit abides.

Great Spirit, Ancient Ones, I thank you for your guidance and ask that you watch over me until the circle is empowered again. So be it.

Finally, when all is said and done, sit down and eat some raw vegetables and bread, and drink some fruit juice. Magic takes personal energy, and it may leave you a little light-headed. Taking time to eat also grounds out any excess energy, neatly putting your feet back on the ground—especially important if you're driving anywhere afterward!

The Solitary Path

Not everyone who chooses the Wiccan Path can find a group with which to study and practice. And some people simply prefer their spiritual efforts to remain a private affair. If you find yourself in either category, consider initiating yourself to the Craft through a ritual like the one that follows.

In Latin, the word *initiate* means "to enter into" or "begin." Similarly, *dedication* refers to both a declaration and a consecration. So initiation represents an important step. This rite declares your intentions to the Universal Powers. It also consecrates your promise to begin making Wiccan tenets an integral part of your thoughts and actions.

Initiation starts you on a philosophical road that leads to spiritual growth and enlightenment. But you should not enter into such a commitment without serious thought. Meditate on what exactly Wicca means. If after so doing you feel an assurance deep within that Wicca is the right path for you, then proceed with confidence and joy.

Ritual of Self-Dedication

Preparation

Make or obtain some type of special ritual garb. Have two white candles on the altar, to represent intentions, and one central candle that represents you. Burn sandalwood incense for cleansing and intuition. Place any images of the Divine that have personal meaning on the altar, if you wish. Gather whatever tools you plan to use regularly as part of your Wiccan practice. Have a small bottle of anointing oil prepared from personally significant ingredients.

The Ritual Bath

For this observance I recommend a ritual bath in which you wash away the old, and welcome the new. Add herbs to the bathwater— perhaps rose for perfect love, nutmeg for tenacity, mint to improve your meditative state, violet for peace and purpose, lemon for cleansing, and ginger for power. As you soak in the tub, breathe deeply to release your tensions, and ponder what this ritual means to you. When you're done, put on your ritual robe, leaving any "mundane" trappings such as watches in the bathroom.

Sacred Space

Invoke the four quarters of the magic circle to watch over you in this ritual. One possible invocation for this purpose is:

EAST

Guardians of the Air, breathe lightly on me with the winds of change, and watch this place as I take the first step along the path of magic.

SOUTH

Guardians of the Fire, burn ever within. Watch this place and ignite the sparks of magic that already abide in my heart.

WEST

Guardians of the Water, saturate my spirit. Watch this place, bringing with you the waves of inspiration to guide my soul.

NORTH

Guardians of the Earth, grant me roots. Watch this place, bringing with you the rich soil in which my new life may grow.

In this case, the invocation to the Spirit will wait until the next part of the ritual.

The Dedication

Now go to the area in which you've assembled your altar and tools. Light the two white candles to represent the presence of the God and Goddess, saying: *"With the lighting of these candles I welcome the Divine to hear my words and witness the intentions of my heart."*

Light the chosen incense, saying: *"Let the smoke that rises carry with it my prayers to walk in perfect love and trust along the path of beauty."*

Light the central candle of self, saying: *"The flame of this candle is my questing spirit, seeking after reunion with the Old Ones. May it burn brightly, chasing any shadows and illuminating my path, which I now declare as Wicca. From this day forward I dedicate myself to living the magic, in word and deed."*

Take your bottle of oil. Put some on your fingertip and touch it to your body where noted, reciting the request that follows:

Forehead "May my spirit grow with insight and wisdom."
Eye "May I see truth and beauty in all things."

Mouth "May my words be gentle, yet filled with power."
Heart "May I be open to freely give and receive love."
Stomach "May my instincts be sound."
Feet "May my magical path be grounded, yet ever growing. So
   mote it be."

Next, place your strong hand (the one you write with) over
your magical tools. Close your eyes, visualizing the white light of
the Spirit pouring into and through you into the tools, saying:
*"Guardians, Great Spirit, Old Ones, heed the prayer of one seeking
your blessings. Cleanse and empower these tools that they might
become implements for positive magic in my hands. I claim each for
my workings, knowing that by your grace I enable their potential. By
your power, through my will, so be it."*

Take a few moments now to look at your tools, consider their
symbolism, and hold them so they absorb more of your personal
energy. Linger for a while in the sacred space, making notes of
your experience and your feelings today in a journal. Reread this
entry annually on the anniversary of this occasion to see how
much you've grown, and to celebrate the new magical being you
become each day.

Closing the Circle

Now all that remains is to thank and release the guardians.

WEST
*Powers of the West, I thank you for your time and inspiration. As I
go from this sacred space, empower my magic so that it flows freely
in and around my life.*

SOUTH
*Powers of the South, I thank you for your time and energy. As I go
from this sacred space, empower my magic so that it may ever burn
as a source of encouragement in my heart.*

EAST

Powers of the East, I thank you for your time and energy. As I go from this sacred space, empower my magic with your creative winds so that it may ever be a source of hope in my heart.

NORTH

Powers of the North, I thank you for your time and energy. As I go from this sacred space, empower my magic with solid foundations so that it may grow daily in my heart.

CENTER

Great Spirit, I thank you for attending this space and witnessing this first step on my spiritual sojourn. Be with me, guiding my magical path, and watch over me until I return to the circle again. So be it.

Blow out the two white candles, but leave yours burning until it goes out naturally. If necessary, move it to a fire-safe location. This represents the fact that magic is not limited to the ritual space; you carry it with you always.

Wiccan Rule Book

In Wicca, personal culpability is very important. Because you have taken on the role of priest or priestess, the responsibility for the power you raise and direct lies solely in your lap. Consequently, while the Wiccan Redes are not carved in stone, most practitioners agree that following the precepts listed here makes for the most responsible, fulfilling, and empowering magical experiences:

1. Never work magic that can potentially harm anyone, including yourself. Release the energy raised during rituals with the phrase, "For the greatest good, and it harm none," to help ensure the best possible results.

2. Never seek to manipulate others with magic. The rule of "do unto others" is a good one to follow in considering your motivations. Remember, whatever energy you send out returns threefold.

3. Recognize your limits. Avoid working any magic when you are ill, angry, tired, harried, or tense. No matter how experienced a practitioner you may be, these mental and physical states can negatively effect your magic.

4. Listen to the small voice within for guidance. Never enact a ritual, spell, prayer, or invocation that you don't understand, or one that includes parts with which you're uncomfortable. Either personalize the exercise, or find another whose actions and words mirror your heart and path.

5. Be true to yourself. When working in groups, never let *anyone* tell you that you *must* do something that goes against a personal taboo or moral code. Groups or individuals that do this seek to manipulate others instead of teaching in perfect love and trust. Politely decline participating in such a spell or ritual, and begin looking for another group with which to work regularly.

6. Recognize your innate potential. Working alone or using un-complicated spells and rituals does not decrease the potential power of your magic. One person who believes wholly in his or her potential outweighs twenty who just go through the motions with-out real meaning. Likewise, personally designed spells and rituals that are kept simple often carry more energy than intricate ones. Your understanding holds the magic in focus, not the intricacy.

7. Let your magic grow with you. Unlike some religious traditions, Wiccan ideas about how to wield your magic, and live your life should not remain static. Every gathering, every book you read, every life experience affects your beliefs somehow. Faith is the cornerstone of magic—faith in yourself and in Universal Powers. So take time out periodically to ascertain changes in your beliefs, and then find positive ways to integrate them into your ritual practices.

Family Festival Album

While the rituals in the remaining pages of this book were written for a person working alone, my hope is that everyone can share them with others by making minor changes. But in either case, as you commemorate the Wiccan Wheel and other special moments in your life, keep a record of these festivities. Make notes about how you personalized the events, take pictures, encourage the participants to write up their special memories from the day, and keep these all together in a binder. Then, as these occasions come up again, you can return to your collection for ideas and inspiration.

PART II

The Wiccan Wheel

Come when the heart beats high and warm
with banquet song, and dance, and wine.
—Fitz-Greene Halleck

2

Candlemas: February 2

In New York, the snows of winter still lie abundantly on the doorstep. I find myself yearning for the warmth of spring as Candlemas arrives, reminding me that reprieve is just around the corner. As the name implies, Candlemas honors the element of Fire, and the sun's slow return to power in the sky. Yet, because winter still lingers with a chilly air, this is not a showy celebration. It is one of thoughtfulness, of finding the light that resides within us. The theses of this holiday are contemplation, providence, health, opportunity, and change.

The Irish celebrate the Feast of Brigid today. Brigid was the goddess of creativity, especially home crafts. Her domain also includes agriculture and protecting baby animals. In the home of the gods, heroes ate and drank from Brigid's cauldron, and it never ran out of sustenance. Throughout Ireland people decorated her sacred wells, decorated their homes with rushes or corn and oats, and offered her ale at the feast.

The Aztec New Year also falls on this date; it is a time to purify and fortify the fields for planting. As an interesting corollary, Candlemas was once called Imbolc, meaning "in the womb," implying a period of gestation. The sun's growing rays begin generating life beneath the soil now. This gives Candlemas a special focus on unseen potentialities, and banishing your inner shadows.

Preparations

Gather together as many light sources as possible. Suggestions include white candles, flashlights, incense sticks, and small oil lamps for indoor gatherings. Outdoors, consider torches or a well-tended bonfire.

For the activities in this ritual you will need: some ice or snow; a cauldron or cup of soil and a seed; your personal journal and a pen; ale or buttered toast for an offering; corn husks for decoration; and any white items. This is Brigid's color as the Maiden aspect of the Goddess.

The Altar

Arrange your light sources in a pleasing manner around the ritual space, but leave them dark. The center of the altar holds a coal or other fire source from your hearth or that of the group's leader. It is the only thing burning at the start of the ritual. Next to the fire source, leave a container of ice or snow. On the other side place your seed, the soil, and dish.

Corn husks are scattered on the surface of the altar like a cloth. Your personal journal and pen sit at one corner. The offering of toasted bread or ale rests on the other corner.

Invocation

Before starting the invocation, go to your door and open it, saying, *"Brigid, I welcome you to our sacred space. As you enter, bring with you the fires of warmth and fertility."* Traditions similar to this are very old, the opening of the door symbolically making way for the powers of light.

Go to the center and pick up the sacred fire. As you walk the circle reciting the invocation, begin igniting the light sources in that quarter of the room. This creates the visual effect of the circle of magic coming alive around you.

EAST

I welcome the Air, and the rising sun. Let the light-filled wind bring inspiration and the breeze of new beginnings.

SOUTH

I welcome the Fire, and the noonday sun. Let the purifying light of the Spirit bring energy and courage with which to walk my path daily.

WEST

I welcome the Water, and the setting sun. Let the twilight bring thoughtfulness and wisdom to my magic.

NORTH

I welcome the Earth, and the resting sun. Let the moment of fertile darkness give my soul peace, and my magic foundations."

CENTER

Light the God and Goddess candles now from the sacred flame. "I welcome the Spirit of ever-burning truth and light. Let your fires be ever present in my mind, my heart, and my magic."

Meditation and Visualization

Sit in the center of the light generated around the room. Look at the flame of the sacred fire until you can see it in your mind's eye clearly. Close your eyes and breathe deeply, continuing to visualize that flame. See it slowly growing in power and beauty until the fire encompasses your whole being, restoring strength, health, and insight.

Once you feel the energy of that light filling you to overflowing, shift your awareness. See yourself as you sit right now, with light shining all around you. Slowly shrink that light down into one brilliant spark that resides in your heart chakra, banishing any shadows that hide within. This ember of the Spirit, this light of truth is always with you, empowering and guiding your magic.

Sit quietly pondering the significance of light in your magic and everyday life, and—when you feel ready—open your eyes and make note of any insights in your journal. Then continue with the ritual. (Note: if this meditation is done in a group, one person should talk the others through it so the group finishes together.)

The Ritual

Stand in place, raise your hands toward the sacred altar, close your eyes, and whisper this chant three times: *"The Goddess in me, in my understanding. The Goddess in me, in my heart. The Goddess in me, in my spirit. The light in me, in my body. The light in me, in my mind. The light in me, in my soul."* Put your arms down, open your eyes, and say, *"I welcome the light."*

Walk up to the altar now and, taking the container of soil and seed in hand, raise it to the heavens. *"This soil of Earth is also the soil of my spirit. Today I plant the seed of* _____ [fill in with a quality that you wish to develop] *in this loam to be warmed by the returning sun, and grown with love."* Plant the seed in the soil, and put the container in front of you on the altar.

Take the container of partially melted snow or ice and raise it upward, saying, *"This is the Water of the Maiden who returns to Earth today, generating life and fertility with her warmth."* Pour the melted snow into the container with the soil and the seed. *"This Water shall likewise nourish the seed of* _____ *now growing in my soul."* Pour the remaining liquid out to Earth as a libation. If this ritual takes place indoors, save the snow or ice until the circle is closed, then take it outside. After the ritual, the soil and seed should be transferred into a large pot and placed in a sunny window to activate the magic.

Other Activities

Even in ancient days this festival included a time for omen observation, specifically to figure out the weather to come. That's how Groundhog Day got started! So consider taking a walk outside to see what signs you can discern from Nature's storehouse of wisdom.

A great activity for kids is making their own Imbolc candles. All you need for this is melted wax, a wick, and an old milk carton that acts as a mold. Allow the kids to add any powdered herbs or aromatic oils they wish, then keep this safely stored away for next year's festivities.

Closing the Circle

NORTH

Under the moonlight the resting Earth lay until the dawn brings a new birth.

WEST

The Waters recede with a setting sun, but the magic continues when the circle is done.

SOUTH

The Fires die down, the candles go out, but within my heart there lingers no doubts.

EAST

The Air calms, but the breath of Spirit remains. Merry part, and merry meet again.

Instead of dismissing the center point, go to your door again, taking with you the toasted bread. Toss the bread out the door for the birds, saying, *"Accept this gift of bread to nourish the children of the winds as my thanks to you, Brigid, for your presence...for sharing the fire from your hearth to bless, inspire, and heal me. May I keep these embers safely burning in my heart."* Close the door. *"So be it."*

When disassembling the Candlemas altar, make sure to save

one corn husk or sheaf of wheat. Wrap it in white cloth and put it in a safe place until next year to bring providence.

Postritual Foods

Any seed items can symbolize new beginnings and fertility. For example, bake spiced pumpkin or sunflower seeds—the spices considered representative of the sun's warmth.

In group settings, it's fun to have a postritual ale-brewing party. Once it's made, each person can take home a bottle and tend it as a symbol of the group's unity. Then next Candlemas, the ale can be served during the ritual to honor Brigid.

3

Imbolc Ritual

Preparations

Three women are needed for this ritual, one to represent the Maiden, the second the Mother, and the last the Crone. All the people attending the ritual should bring candles with them. Additionally you will need evergreens, bundles of wheat (one for each participant), a twelve-inch black ribbon, a white flower tied with ribbon, a wand, four white candles at the quarter points, a cauldron placed in the south with a white candle inside, a dark shawl, a bouquet of flowers, a broom, and a white taper.

The Altar

Cover the altar with a white cloth and edge it with evergreens to represent life in the midst of death. Place the white flower and the wand together in the center of the altar. These are figuratively called the "Bride's Bed." Alongside them lay out the bundles of wheat decoratively, the shawl, floral bouquet, and white taper. Lean the broom at one side.

Invocation

Purely personal.

Meditation and Visualization

None given, but an appropriate one can be added. Read over the ritual before you design suitable materials.

The Ritual

The three women chosen stand around the altar, saying the following three times:

> *The Maiden comes to bring us light;*
> *the winter dies, and all is bright.*
> *The frozen ground shall disappear*
> *and all shall sprout, for spring is near.*

Each woman takes up the symbol of her role in the ritual: the Crone dons the shawl, the Maiden takes up the bouquet, and the Mother picks up the white candle. The woman portraying the Mother says:

> *Behold the threefold Goddess,*
> *Maiden, Mother, and Crone.*
> *She is one; she is three; together and alone.*
> *Summer comes not without spring;*
> *without summer, comes no winter chill;*
> *without winter, spring is not born;*
> *the three, life's cycles fulfill.*
> *Let us celebrate Imbolc!*

The Maiden picks up the broom and sweeps the circle counterclockwise. This frees the space of all that is old. While she sweeps, the Maiden says:

With this broom filled with power,
Sweep away the old and sour,
Sweep away the chill of death,
Winter draws its last cold breath.
Round, round, round about,
Sweep the old and useless out!

The Maiden now takes up the bundles of straw and gives one to each participant in the circle, explaining that these represent winter and death. All participants channel any lingering negativity into their bundles, which will later be burned to release it.

After this, the Crone lights the candle in the cauldron. She collects each person's bundle, ties them all together with the black ribbon, and sets it on fire, saying:

Thus we melt the winter; and warm the breath of spring.
We bid adieu to what is dead; and greet each living thing.
Thus we banish winter; thus we welcome spring!

The Maiden collects into a basket the candles that all participants have brought. She places this on the altar. The Mother then says:

I bless these creatures of wax and light,
casting out all negativity.
Serve your purpose, flaming bright,
infused with magic, you shall be.
Instruments of light and strength,
wick and wax though you may be,
I give you life of needed length
to aid in creativity!
So mote it be.

The Maiden then returns the candles to all participants.

Other Activities

Allow all participants in the circle to say what they are burning in the Imbolc fires, and what they claim in its place. Once each participant has told the group what he or she claims, the others present repeat this word three times by way of affirmation. For example, if Mary desires peace, the group chants together, "Peace, peace, peace." This directs the energy of peace to Mary's body, mind, and spirit.

Another potential activity is a blessing of cakes and ale, shared around the circle to represent continued providence.

Closing the Circle

The leader of the group speaks the following while walking the circle counterclockwise slowly, ending in the center for the prayer to the Bride.

As we close this Celebration of Imbolc, let each of us find joy in the power of the returning sun. As each new day dawns, and the light becomes brighter and stronger, remember that your inner light should burn as brightly. Feel the changes in Earth around you as winter recedes and Earth sprouts with new life. Remember the wonder you felt as you awakened from youth to adulthood. Relive the joy of that awakening and heal any scars you have. Breathe deeply of the harmony of Earth's new life and rejoice in your own!

Dearest Bride, Maiden of all that is fresh and new, we warmly thank you for attending our Rite of Imbolc. As this circle is dissolved, we ask that you guide us in our new beginnings and inspire us with fresh creativity. Hail and farewell!"

4

Spring Equinox: March 21

The windows crack open for the first time since late fall, letting in fresh, cherry-blossom-scented air that plays in every corner of my home. I sit quietly in the dining room during the early-morning hours, savoring the quiet, the aromas, and the sunlight dancing through stained glass. Spring has finally come.

Easter, which takes place around this date, takes its name from the ancient goddess Eostre. Her color is yellow, the hue of early-sprouting plants. Traditionally, Esotre received eggs as an offering—a mark of her fertile nature. The themes of this holiday are liberation, the Air element, and new beginnings.

I, like the ancients, find this to be a miraculous moment of awakening. Everything on Earth shows signs of life and potential, including the seeds planted at Candlemas. The world is fruitful and the child within all of us has reason to rejoice. Today, light and darkness are equal; then the Sun God begins his ascent to power.

Preparations

To prepare the ritual space, burn incense (such as orange bergamot, lavender, lily, mint, or sage); use a handheld fan or large feather to disperse it as you walk. Have a tape or CD with flute music (or any other wind instrument) playing in the background. Turning a fan onto LOW adds to the ambience if no natural winds are present.

A cauldron or cup is again filled with rich soil. Also have ready a rectangular planter, the seedling from Candlemas, and four stones, one for each element. For Earth use green agate, coal, green jasper, or salt. For Air use aventurine, pumice, or mica. For Fire use red agate, amber, bloodstone, or carnelian. For Water use blue agate, amethyst, coral, or lapis.

If you have an outdoor garden where you can work, hold the ritual outside instead of having a planter at the altar. Anoint yourself with patchouli oil to honor the Fire element. If possible, perform the ritual at dawn, the time of beginnings. Finally, into the ritual carry a raw egg and leave it on the altar as a symbol of spring fertility.

The Altar

Cover the altar with a yellow cloth, honoring the Air element and Eostre. Prepare a bowl of fragrant petals from early-blossoming flowers and small feathers (try a craft store to find these), and leave it on one corner of the altar. On the other, place a string of tiny bells. Pale green candles are a good choice for divine representations, because this is the color of new plant growth.

Invocation

Pick up the bowl of flower petals and feathers, and begin walking the circle, sprinkling them along the perimeter. Stop at each compass point, lighting an appropriately scented stick of incense at each quarter point as you invoke that power.

EAST

Sylphs and Spirits of the Winds, I call to you. Come to this place with the ancient song of air on your wings.

SOUTH

Salamanders and Spirits of Fire, I call to you. Come to this place to warm the winds of spring and give life to the magic.

WEST

Undines and Spirits of Water, I call to you. Come to this place with salty sea air that motivates the tides of inspiration.

NORTH

Gnomes and Spirits of Earth, I call to you. Come to this place with the living magic that abides in each grain of soil, and within my soul.

CENTER

Guardians and Great One, I call to you. Come to this place with creation's power. Bind the elements into one and bear the magic safely to its mark.

Meditation and Visualization

Envision a wheel of spinning starlight; you sit at the vortex. It slowly moves clockwise. The cold, silvery stars transform into tiny green buds and sprouts. The scene around you teems with life, with the smell of new grass, early flowers, and the sounds of robins, which bear the spring on their wings.

Feel the rhythm of the season beating with your heart. Hear spring breezes in your breath. Smell the newness in your own aura. Earth has thrown off winter's cloak, yet you are not cold. The sun instead embraces you, fills you, and holds you in this place between worlds.

As the light saturates every cell, let all your tension and any sickness fill the egg you've carried. Whisper to the egg of things that you wish, of abilities you want to hone. Also place within its shell those things that bind you. Leave them there; your spirit no longer needs such constraints. Let it fly free with the winds of spring.

When you feel finished, open your eyes, and make notes of your impressions in your journal. Then, continuing to carry the egg, start the main part of the ritual.

The Ritual

Stand before the altar. Hold your hands, palms down, over the string of bells. Close your eyes and repeat this chant until it naturally grows loud, then quiets into silence: *"Winter recedes, spirits are freed; darkness take to flight, spring winds, fill with light."* Take a moment to just stand here, absorbing the energy created by chanting.

Next, take out the egg you carry. Hold it cupped in both hands, saying: *"Bonds are broken, by potential replaced; sickness shall cease, the magic's released."* Break the egg to symbolize your spiritual rebirth. Place in the bowl to give to a pet cat or dog, or to mingle with the soil in the next part of the ritual so the negatives can grow into something positive.

Finally, take out the four stones you've chosen to represent the elements. Begin placing them in the four corners of the planter (or your garden) saying, *"Earth is alive and fertile. The winds blow the seeds to the soil* [East/Air]; *the Sun God gives warmth* [South/Fire]; *the Rain Goddess nourishes* [West/Water]; *the Earth roots* [North/ Earth]. Pour the soil from the cauldron into the planter (or your garden), gently place the seedling in the center, then hold both hands over it. *"Let my spirit be as this seedling, flexible to the winds of change, ever reaching toward the sun, inspired to grow by the rain, and grounded solidly in my path."*

After the ritual, keep this planter in a sunny window, where you can tend and nurture your spirit with the seedling. If you used your garden, make sure it receives plenty of water. Whenever possible, meditate quietly with this plant nearby; Nature spirits have much to teach us when we learn to listen.

Other Activities

Because one of the themes of this day is restoring balance, make yourself a special charm to represent symmetry out of opposites. Gather together a white stone and a black stone, a feather (for the sky) and some soil (for the Earth), a two-toned cloth, and a piece of string. At sunset, place the items in the center of the cloth. Gather the ends of the cloth and tie them with the string. As you do so, repeat this incantation three times, each time making a knot to bind the magic: *"Poised between Earth and sky, moon and sun, now the magic is begun."* Carry this anytime you feel a portion of your life is getting out of balance.

Another activity entails taking pieces of grain and rubbing them on every doorway and window in your home. According to Peruvian custom, this protects the inhabitants from misfortune. Or you can tie wishes in the form of ribbons loosely to a tree so the winds can loose them and release the magic.

This is an excellent day to perform any Blessingways, Birth Rites, and children's rituals, too.

Closing the Circle

Since this ritual focuses on the Air element, it will be the last one dismissed becfore the Spirit. So the closing begins in the north.

NORTH
Gnomes and Spirits of the Land, I thank you for your fruitful energy. Carry peace and renewal from this place through the roots of trees, and on the breath of beasts.

WEST
Undines and Spirits of the Water, I thank you for your flowing energy. Carry peace and renewal from this place in every drop of rain, and on every wave that caresses the shores.

SOUTH
*Salamanders and Spirits of the Fire, I thank you for your motivating
energy. Carry peace and renewal from this place in every ray of
sunshine that touches Earth.*

EAST
*Sylphs and Spirits of the Air, I thank you for your billowing energy.
Carry peace and renewal from this place in every wind and breeze,
in the sound of bells, and on the wings of birds.*

CENTER
*Guardians and Great One, I thank you for your blessed energy.
Carry renewal from this place with every star wished upon. Release
in me my inner child, loose any bondage, and grant my spirit the
wings of peace. So be it.*

When the circle is closed, take the string of bells that has been
charged by your ritual to a nearby window. Hang them here,
where their gentle music announces the winds of change and the
never-ending turning of the Wiccan Wheel.

Postritual Foods

All egg dishes are perfectly suited to spring, being symbols of
fertility. Make scrambled eggs for breakfast, an egg salad sandwich
for lunch, a quiche for dinner, and deviled eggs for snacks! Other
prolific foods include a sliced cucumber and carrot salad, date nut
bread, and rice.

Consider making hot cross buns. These represent the Wheel of
the Year and the solar disk. Preserving one in the house keeps all
within from ever wanting for food. In Russia people serve small
pancakes with butter to represent the sun, accompanied by vodka
with a twist of lemon (vodka equals fire; lemon equals the yellow
of the solar disk).

5

Beltane: May 1

But I must gather knots of flowers,
and buds and garlands gay.
—Alfred, Lord Tennyson

When I was a child, my friends and I took to nearby fields early on Beltane morning and gathered wildflowers. We placed these decoratively in handwoven baskets, then left them anonymously on doorsteps. I suspect all the neighbors knew who the gifts came from, but they didn't mind. It was a random act of beauty and innocent fun, and nearly as lovely a surprise as the abundant blossoms of May themselves.

The Festival of May Eve is an ancient rite, marking winter's official ending. It is an unbridled celebration of fertility of the Earth, and in humans. The centerpoint of most May Day celebrations, the May pole, represents the phallus; the ribbons are the feminine aspect and the weaving of fate. When you consider the life spans of our ancestors, it's easy to see why this would be such an important celebration.

Beltane marks a point on the Wiccan Wheel when the boundary between this world and other dimensions is thin.

Fairies take advantage of this condition by joining us in the May Day observances. The themes of this holiday are fertility, ecology, illumination, and passion.

Preparations

Find a tape or CD of Celtic music to play in the background. According to Scottish tradition, this keeps all evil at bay. Decorate the sacred space with plentiful flowers, ribbons, and bright colors.

The night before, extinguish your hearth fire (or stove pilot light). Leave this out until during or after the ritual. If possible, gather rainwater or dew at this time. Use this in the altar bowl; it brings inner beauty.

For the ritual itself, you will need: a symbol of winter (perhaps a white sachet stuffed with winter spices); three ribbons bound together at one end (choose the color according to things you want to weave into your life); a slice of buttered oat bread; a brazier of fire; a covered fire source (or small lamp); and a long match.

The Altar

Cover the altar with a green cloth to honor the Earth Mother. Sprinkle marigold flowers on top. Have ready a bowl filled with thyme, oak leaves, ash leaves, and straw pieces; with this you will mark the circle. Secure the ribbons to the middle of the altar's surface so you can braid them during the ritual. The effigy of winter goes on one side of the altar. On the other are a bowl of water and another receptacle into which you can pour it.

Invocation

This invocation begins in the south to honor Fire. As you begin, pick up the bowl of leaves from the altar and scatter them around. These herbs are sacred to the fairy-folk and will help draw their energy into the circle.

which you meditated, as a gift of thanks to the fairies. If you can't do this, just leave it outside for the birds. As they eat, they will take your appreciation on their wings.

Postritual Foods

Try red foods for love and the Fire element. The traditional May bowl consists of wine in which strawberries and woodruff float. In Celtic tradition, oat cakes were made with charms inside, each symbol foretelling the recipient's future. Oatmeal cookies are a good alternative.

6

Summer Solstice: June 21

Summer Solstice arrives at my home to mixed emotions. The humidity permeates everything as the sun beats down on the pavement. It seems reprieve from the heat is nowhere to be found. Yet in just a few short months it will be cold again, so we spend as much time outside as possible, usually at the barbecue. My friends jokingly say that cooking at the grill is my personal Fire Ritual; they don't know how right they are.

Magically, Summer Solstice brings us to the halfway point of the Wheel of the Year. The sun reigns fully, reaching a peak in the sky, and shedding beams of truth. We can't look directly at the sun's brilliance, yet its light allows us to see things clearly, banishes our shadows, and releases the past. The themes of Summer Solstice are sex, love, creativity, energy, luck, health, and wishes.

Many practitioners harvest their magical herbs on Midsummer's Eve. The timing increases the herbs' potency. Should you choose to do likewise, cut the herbs with a special knife (but never one made of iron, which banishes magic) and leave an offering of honey to the plant in thankfulness. Remember, the path of Wicca always leads to walking in reciprocity with Nature.

Preparations

Add summer flowers to your ritual bath, and anoint yourself with their oils before the ritual. For the ritual itself, you will need a fire source, your favorite divination tool, some dew or rainwater from the night before, one stick of protective incense for every room in your house, a white candle, and a sun wheel.

Fashion the latter from grapevines or rose briers so the branches form a circle with an equidistant cross in the center. Decorate this with golden ribbons and symbols of the four elements. Gather together nine dried herbs in a bowl, each of which represents a personal (or group) need or goal. Nine is the number of completion.

The Altar

Cover the altar with a red or orange cloth to honor the sun. Decorate the top with daisy blossoms. The daisy takes its name from *day's-eye,* because it turns to follow the sun in its path. Use gold, yellow, or red candles to represent divine Fire. Place your fire source at the center of the altar with your divination tool in front of it, the sun wheel and water at one side, and the bowl of herbs, white candle, and incense on the other.

Invocation

If possible, this ritual should begin at noon, when the sun is highest in the sky. A nice additional touch for this invocation is to have candles at all four compass points to represent the dominance of the Fire element.

SOUTH
Fires of Creation, within me burn,
for the Wheel of Life has turned.
Keep safe the sun's dynamic spark;
Throughout the world, ignite the dark.

WEST

Waters of Creation, within me flow;
'round again the Wheel must go.
Keep safe the dew of dusk and dawn;
let magic prance upon the lawn.

NORTH

Loam of Fertility, nourish me;
the Wheel's lessons I wish to see.
Keep safe the soil where roots can grow,
while round the circle, magic sows!

EAST

Air of Insight, breathe in this place;
the Wheel of Time shall guide your pace.
Keep safe the winds of muse and mind;
within this circle, the magic bind.

CENTER

Spirit of Truth, and psychic power,
the Wheel has turned again this hour.
Keep safe the light that warms the land;
birth the magic where I stand.

If your fire source is not already burning, light it now along with the God and Goddess candles.

Meditation and Visualization

At the altar, take your divination tool in your weak hand. Dip the pointer finger of your strong hand into the water and draw an invoking pentagram in the air above the tool, saying: *"Powers of Insight, I invoke you. Let the power of light this day grant me sight beyond sight. Reveal the patterns of the Wheel as it turns, and the lessons I must learn."* Repeat this procedure on your forehead with the water and the invocation, then sit down with your tool.

Hold the divination tool in your hands and close your eyes. Open your senses and breathe deeply. Visualize the light in your aura filling the tool, and the energy of the tool filling your aura. This attunes your auric energy to that of the tool, and vice versa. Continue this visualization until the tool feels warm and welcoming in your hands.

Open your eyes and proceed with a reading. If possible, draw out six emblems to represent the trends over the next six months. Make notes of this reading in your journal and return to it at Yule to see how accurate it was.

The Ritual

Stand before the altar and take the bowl of herbs in hand, saying: *"Fires of Fertility, sun of creation, I welcome you. As these herbs burn, let their smoke carry the message of my needs swiftly to your hearth, and gather there the light of magic."* Begin sprinkling the nine herbs on the fire source, one at a time, saying:

> *On the count of one, the spell's begun.*
> *On the count of two, my wishes come true.*
> *On the count of three, the magic's freed.*
> *On the count of four, I open the door.*
> *On the count of five, the magic's alive.*
> *On the count of six, the magic, affix!*
> *On the count of seven, it reaches the heavens.*
> *On the count of eight, no more to wait.*
> *On the count of nine, what I wish is mine!*

Afterward, move yourself through the smoke created by these herbs three times for mental, physical, and spiritual health throughout the rest of the year.

Next, light a white candle from the flames before you and take it to a room in your house. From this fire, ignite a stick of protective incense, raise it before you, and invoke your household god's and/or goddess's blessing. Leave the incense burning (in a proper container); repeat this in every room of your house. This cleanses your home and safeguards it against negativity, especially malintentioned magic.

At the end of your ritual, pick up the sun wheel and hold it to your heart. Close your eyes and make a wish. Make this wish as specific as possible, and visualize it in completed form. Then release that energy to your fire source by tossing in the sun wheel. The fire inspires manifestation. Let this burn itself out naturally, or douse it with the divining water.

Alternatively, make your wish and hang the sun wheel in a visually predominant part of your home. Each time you see it, repeat your wish, until it manifests. Then take down the wheel and keep it safely put away for next year's ritual.

Other Activities

This is an excellent time of year to make protective charms for your home or pets. For this, gather together a piece of rowan wood, red fabric, and red thread. If you wish, add other warding herbs, such as St. John's wort, woodbine, vervain, anise, or salt to the mixture. Bundle the herbs in the cloth. Gather it at the top, saying: *"Where rowan and red are bound, protection surrounds."* Each time you say this, make one knot in the red thread. Put the charm in any safe place around your home; it can also be kept in the glove compartment of a car.

Traditionally, this is also an excellent day to cast spells to attract a lover, or refresh a relationship. My favorite spell for either purpose begins by gathering rose petals at dawn, the time of hope. Whisper your desire into the petals, then release them to the winds during your ritual. Their fragrance carries your wish to the intended person.

Closing the Circle

Stand in the center of your circle, facing east. Turn slowly counterclockwise, saying, *"Turn, turn, turn, the Wheel must turn. As*

dawn to day, as day to night, so the Wheel turns, filled with might."
End in the east and start dismissing the quarters.

EAST

*Wind of Change, move on, move on. With the ever-turning Wheel,
go from this place carrying the air of magic.*

NORTH

*Loam of Earth, move on, move on. With the ever-turning Wheel, go
from this place planting the seeds of magic.*

WEST

*Water of Birth, move on, move on. With the ever-turning Wheel, go
from this place, cresting with waves of magic.*

SOUTH

*Fires of Creation, move on, move on. With the ever-turning Wheel,
go from this place, burning with the embers of magic.*

CENTER

*Spirit of light, move on, move on. With the ever-turning Wheel, go
from this place, empowering the energy of magic.*

Postritual Foods

Try any hot-flavored foods—such as curry dishes, stuffed onions,
or stuffed peppers—and items baked in the oven (the hearth fire)
to which solar spices are added.

Also consider having a barbecue to honor the Fire element.

7

Lammas: August 1

During late summer my family took trips to the Adirondack Mountains to visit my grandmother. The drive was long and arduous, but filled with beautiful sights. We always arrived during the wee hours of morning, and fell immediately into bed. Without fail, shortly after 8:00 A.M., the smell of fresh-baked bread coaxed us out of the comfort of bed to the breakfast table. I can't say for sure if Grandma knew about the tradition of making Lammas bread, but the memory remains a luscious one.

Lammas celebrates the first harvest—often that of wild edibles and early-ripening cultivated foods such as apples. Specifically Lammas honors the Grain Spirit, as the giver and preserver of life. Consequently, Wiccans frequently observe this day by baking bread, rolls, or cookies for during or after the ritual.

Additionally, an ancient version of Lammas was dedicated to Lugh, the god of mastery and craftsmanship. With this in mind, your ritual tools can be cleansed and blessed today, along with any other implements of personal arts. Once the ritual has ended, it is an excellent day to work on something creative! The themes of Lammas are community, money, providence, manifestation, and agriculture.

Preparations

Use oatmeal soap as part of your ritual bath. Fashion a Corn Maiden from dried husks and keep this to decorate your altar every year so your household will never want for food. Staying with this theme, have a bowl of dried loose grain to sprinkle around the circle during the invocation. This brings prosperity, protection, and fertility.

The Altar

Cover the altar with an orange-colored cloth. Decorate the surface with sheafs of grain, wheat, and crab apples. Add a bundle of Indian corn as an alternative God emblem and a loaf of corn bread for the Goddess. Place the bowl of grain at one side of the surface, your seedling from Candlemas at the other; in the center, place a small bowl with a teaspoon of honey and your magical tools or artistic implements.

Also have a brazier of burning charcoal ready, upon which you can place any cleansing herbs you desire.

Invocation

At the altar, pick up the bowl of grain. Disperse this evenly around the circle as you invoke the quarters. I suggest beginning the invocation in the south, since the Wheel has not yet turned to fall. My thanks to David Ledwin for inspiring this adapted piece:

SOUTH
Warm Rays of Sun that nurture seeds to maturity,
I call and charge you.
Let your burning flames forge and temper my spirit
through the smelted fires of creation.
Hail, Fire, hail!

WEST
Warm Water that saturates Earth's seeds to grow,
I call and charge you.
From you am I born, from the ocean's waves

by sea, and spray, and mist.
Hail, Water, hail!

NORTH
Warm Earth that roots seeds in its womb,
I call and charge you.
Let your rich soil grant my spirit sanctuary
in the house of the ancients.
Hail, Earth, hail!

EAST
Warm Airs that carry seeds to the waiting Earth,
I call and charge you.
Let your singing winds fill my heart and soul
with the canticle of the Mysteries.
Hail, Air, hail!

CENTER
Great Spirit who gives life to the seeds,
I call and charge you.
Let your presence bind the elements together
and birth the grains of magic in me.
Hail, Spirit, hail!

Meditation and Visualization

In Scotland, it's customary to pay bills today and make an accounting of finances on Lammas. Following in this tradition, this combination meditation and spell helps draw money to you. When the financial blessing arrives, set it aside for emergency use.

Before beginning the meditation, prepare a dollar bill wrapped three times around with a string. Leave enough string so you can place the money across the table from you. Also find a green candle; carve it with the image of a dollar sign, and put it in the middle of the table.

Light the candle, put the dollar bill across from you with the string in your strong hand, and sit at the table. Center yourself. Observe the candle flame. Use it as a focus. See nothing else;

know the flame to be the same as the one in your heart. Slowly let this image blur, and close your eyes.

Visualize the same brilliant light pouring down from the heavens to shower you with abundance. Change the color to greenish gold, the hue of prosperity. Let this energy fill you to overflowing. When you feel all but ready to burst, allow this power to flow into your fingertips toward the dollar bill across the table. Slowly draw the string into your hands, whispering, *"Money to me; magic fly free,"* until the bill reaches your hands. Wrap the remaining string around the bill, and tuck it into a wallet or purse. Leave the candle to burn down on its own (in a fire-safe container); this will further energize the magic.

When this spell manifests, donate the dollar bill to a worthy cause to show thanks.

The Ritual

Stand before the center of the altar. Sprinkle whatever significant herbs you've chosen on the charcoal. When the smoke begins to rise, lift one of your magical implements and move it through the smoke, saying, *"Today is the first harvest, and I wish to reap magic. Lord of Light, Lady of Creation, bless and charge this tool once again to be used in your service."* Repeat this procedure with each of your regularly used magical implements.

For those who have brought artistic tools to the altar, use this blessing instead: *"Lord of Inspiration and Vision, Lady of Muse, today is the harvest and I wish to reap creativity. Bless and charge this tool for my art that it may ever reflect the growing spirit of light within me."*

Put these items aside, except for your athame (or a pair of scissors if you don't use an athame). Cut a leaf, flower, fruit, or vegetable off the plant you started at Candlemas. Drop a small bit of honey in the soil to thank the plant for its gift. This clipping is about to become your offering of "first fruits."

Place the clipping in the brazier, saying, *"This is my gift to the God of the Sun, and the Lady of Earth. As this burns, so too burns away my* _____." Fill in a bad habit or anything else you need to release, such as a memory from the past. *"In its place, I reap* _____." Fill in an attribute you want to cultivate, or a need you have. *"Teach me to receive nourishment and abundance even as you nourish and fertilize Earth."*

Let this fire burn out of its own accord. As it burns, you may wish to chant this popular circle song, originated by Ian Corrigan:

> *Hoof and horn, hoof and horn,*
> *all that dies shall be reborn.*
> *Corn and grain, corn and grain,*
> *all that falls shall rise again!*

Other Activities

As part of your attire, consider making a corn necklace. Cut fresh corn kernels carefully off the ears so the ends are intact. Pierce each kernel with a threaded needle. Hang the strand in a dry, breezy room and turn the kernels regularly so they dry evenly. Use Indian corn for a more colorful collection. When dried completely, this lasts nearly forever. Longer strands make unique decorations later in the year. Put them on the Yule tree as a symbol of the returning sun.

Another tradition is to begin the process of preserving food for winter today. Perhaps the easiest recipes are those for conserves. Blend together equal parts of sugar and symbolic fruits—perhaps raspberries and oranges, for foresight, abundance, and love. Boil these together until thick, then can them. Keep the blend for use at other gatherings (or for your breakfast toast)!

Closing the Circle

EAST
Lord of the Wind, your seed carries the promise of future harvests from this place. As we sow, so we reap, and sow again. Go in peace.

NORTH

Mother Earth, your bounty sustains and blesses all. Let it nourish my spirit and body until I join you in this sacred space again. Go in peace.

WATER

Lady of the Seas, of the cleansing, nourishing waters, thank you for flowing into this place and my life. Let drops of wisdom within me, as you go in peace.

SOUTH

Lord of the Sun, master of the Fire, thank you for ripening the crops, and maturing my soul. Energize this magic, as you go in peace.

CENTER

Lord and Lady of Creation, thank you for watching over the seeds in the earth, and in my heart. Manifest this magic, as you go in peace.

Postritual Foods

Try homemade breads, and the first fruits and vegetables gathered from your own garden or purchased at a farmer's market, especially apples and zucchini.

8

Autumn Equinox: September 22

The distinct chill of autumn touches the morning air as I ready the children for school. It's dusky outside, but I can still see the brilliance of the trees. The leaves have started to turn red, orange, and gold, mimicking the sun's splendor before they fall to the ground. This is Nature's last dance before resting. I try to take her hint by enjoying as many fresh fruits and vegetables as possible before the homegrown kind disappear from the market.

Abundance coupled with prudence is the theme of the Fall Equinox. While Nature's abundance is reaped, the days begin growing shorter. The increasing scarcity of crops and growing darkness are perhaps why many cultural festivals focus on providence and honoring the dead during the latter part of the year.

Another name for this Wiccan holiday is Mabon. Mabon is the Celtic god of light, and son of the Great Mother. Like Christ, Mabon mediated between humans and the Powers, and eventually sacrificed himself on our behalf. Mabon then descended into the Underworld, metaphorically voyaging into the same darkness that increasingly overwhelms the fall and winter days. The themes for Mabon are reaping, thankfulness, and conservation.

Preparations

Gather one colorful leaf each from rowan, birch, hazel, sassafrass, hawthorn, willow, ash, and oak trees (or as many of those trees as you can find) and wax them prior to the ritual. Store the collection in a white cloth until you're ready to use them.

You will also need a yellow-colored candle to represent the sun and a cup of grape juice or wine. If holding this ritual inside, have a bowl into which you can pour the juice or wine during the rite.

The Altar

Cover the altar with a red or orange (or any color you associate with the harvest) cloth. Decorate the altar with fall fruits and grains, gourds, and bunches of grapes. Add a horn of plenty with coins inside, to the collection.

Place the sun candle at the center of your altar and light it. Keep the goblet of wine just in front of the candle, and put the waxed leaves wrapped to the right or left of center.

Invocation

Since Autumn Equinox marks a change in power from the sun to the moon, begin this invocation in the West. This is the seat of water, traditionally associated with the lunar sphere. It is also the region of the setting sun.

The quarter markers for this invocation could be gourds hand-painted in traditional colors, or those decorated with elemental emblems. For example, use the image of a purple water droplet for the west, a red tongue of flame for the south, a yellow feather for the east, and a brown seed for the north.

In the Greek and Roman traditions, this festival honors Bacchus or Dionysus because of the grape harvest. Consequently I have chosen to call on this deity for the center point of the circle. Feel free to substitute any other god of the harvest with whom you're more familiar.

WEST

Water Maiden, come and celebrate!
  Taste the wine and the fruit filled with your drops.
  Wash gently on the shores of my soul
  with the sustaining waters of creation,
  for I am your servant.

NORTH

Earth Mother, come and celebrate!
  Taste the wine and the fruit of your womb.
  Grow gently in the soils of my soul
  the seeds of Nature's lessons,
  for I am your servant.

EAST

Wind Brother, come and celebrate!
  Taste the wine and fruit of your breath.
  Blow gently into my soul
  with the wind of insight and motivation,
  for I am your servant.

SOUTH

Fire Father, come and celebrate!
  Taste the wine and the fruit you warmed to maturity.
  Burn gently in my heart and soul
  with the empowering embers of magic,
  for I am your servant.

CENTER

Bacchus, Dionysus, come and celebrate!
  Taste the wine and the fruit of Earth's bounty.
  Fill gently my heart and soul
  with the wines of wisdom and wonderment,
  for I am your servant.

Meditation and Visualization

At your altar, take the leaf divination kit in hand. Raise it toward
the sky, saying, "Powers of Light, grant me sight beyond sight. As day

gives way to dark, grant me foresight's inner spark." Sit down and hold the tool in hand. Close your eyes and center your attention on the energy each leaf brings to the bundle. Feel its inherent symbolism in color and form. If any of the leaves seem to have a different meaning to you than those given below, make note of it. Your instincts are important to the divination process; heed their council above anything found in a book.

Now, think about the next three months. Ask Nature's tool what the future holds for you. Keeping your eyes closed, randomly draw out two leaves for each month, placing the first one to your left and the second to your right. The left-hand leaf's symbolism is determined by the one on the right. For example, if you drew maple followed by birch for the month of October, this indicates that your path to inner peace during that time frame lies in activating your feminine attributes. A willow leaf followed by a hawthorn for November indicates that you can achieve your goals then, *if* you learn to be flexible.

Here are the basic correspondences for the leaves:

Rowan Safety; the need for protection
Hazel Wisdom; the use of discernment
Birch Highlights or augments feminine attributes (nurturing, intuition, gentility, and so on)
Maple Peace; truce; reconciliations
Sassafras Physical, spiritual, or emotional well-being
Hawthorn Wishes; goals; desires; achievements
Willow The capacity to bend and change with circumstances
Ash Vitality; energy; power
Oak Highlights or augments masculine attributes (leadership, strength, courage, and so on)

The Ritual

Stand before the center of the altar. Hold your ritual goblet toward the sky with both hands, saying, *"Lord of the Harvest, Lady of*

Crops, I thank you for your gifts freely given, and now return wine from this bounty to the soil with a grateful heart." Pour out the wine to the soil or the secondary container. If you're using the latter, you must take this outside after the ritual and pour it into the earth. *"Accept my offering as a gift to you and Earth. Let this libation nourish and sustain the land as the Wheel moves on."*

Put down the cup, and take up the cornucopia with both hands while reciting: *"Providence, while my table is rich with the harvest, soon the crops fall to the snows. Let each silver piece be used kindly to help others, then return thrice-fold in times of need. Bless these coins that I, and all within my home, might not want for food, nor comfort, while the land lies fallow. By your power, let it be so."* Return the coins to the altar. After the ritual keep them in an accessible place and use them for random acts of kindness, such as putting a quarter into an expired parking meter. Your gifts to others, as the prayer says, will return to you three times over to meet your needs.

"The Wheel has turned. The sun no longer reigns." Blow out the sun candle. *"It is a time of increasing darkness...a time to look within at shadows of my soul and face them bravely. May the Powers be with me in this Underworld journey, that like the sun I will return from my meditations with the brightness of enlightenment as a guide."* Linger before the altar and consider any negatives in your life. Be honest with yourself here. Choose one on which to work for the remainder of the winter so that by Candlemas, it will be banished with growing light.

Other Activities

European tradition says that being hospitable to a stranger on this day brings good luck. Besides this, it is a perfect day for brewing grape wine in honor of Dionysus/Bacchus. To make a gallon, begin with three quarts of water, three pounds of sugar, one 12-ounce can each of white and purple frozen grape juice concentrate (thawed), a sliver of orange peel, a tea bag, and a tablespoon of wine yeast. Put everything except the yeast into a nonaluminum pan and warm it over a medium flame.

When the sugar is totally dissolved, let the mix cool to lukewarm. Meanwhile, mix the yeast with a quarter cup of warm water, which you will stir into the juice after it reaches lukewarm. Cover the pot with a heavy dish towel and leave it for three days to begin the fermenting process. Strain into a glass jug on the third day, but leave the cork very loose for another four weeks. After this time tighten down the cork and store the wine in a cool, dark area. It will be ready to consume within three months—six months if you prefer a drier wine.

Closing the Circle

SOUTH
Fire Father,
may your cooling embers heal heated emotions.
I bid you farewell, with thanks.

EAST
Air Brother,
may your winter winds grant me freshness of mind.
I bid you farewell, with thanks.

NORTH
Earth Mother,
may your providence continue through barrenness.
I bid you farewell, with thanks.

WEST
Water Sister,
may your rains fall freely on parched spirits.
I bid you farewell, with thanks.

CENTER
Spirit of the Vine, of corn and grain,
from you I am born, and shall return again.
I bid you farewell, with thanks.

Postritual Foods

In keeping with the theme of prudence and conservation, serve long-lasting foods such as apples, potatoes, squash, nuts, oats, and onions, or leftovers. Cider and goose are also traditional Autumn Equinox foods.

9

Hallows: October 31

As the children in our neighborhood gleefully don their costumes for Halloween, I cannot help but wonder how many of them know the meaning of their actions. Today is the Celtic New Year and, in what seems to be a dichotomy, it is also the Feast of the Dead.

Because the Wiccan Wheel is ever moving, beginnings and endings are all within its turning. Today the old and new rest on the same ledge, allowing the boundary between this world and the next to grow thin. So while an earthly calendar cycle begins, Wiccans honor the spiritual legacy of those who have passed on to Summerland during this ritual.

Some people believe that what happens on Hallows sets the pace for the entire year to come. So focus on activities and foods that invoke prosperity, joy, and love. It is also a time for giving; find a suitable charity, and volunteer some time or make a donation. This kindness will return to you when most needed. The themes of Hallows are divination, psychichism, death, and transformation.

Preparations

Since spirits and fairies run free today, you may wish to take extra precautions in protecting your home and sacred space. Clean the floors with basil-steeped water to wash away any negativity from the old year. Hang gorse near your windows or doorway, and cast white beans around the circle to banish both ghosts and bad luck.

Gather pictures of, or memorabilia from, people in your life who have passed over, and put these in the sacred space at the western point. For the three other points you will need a knife or scissors, a candle, and a symbol of transformation.

Carve a pair of black and white candles to represent what you want to release and gather for the new year, respectively. Also find a crystal to use for scrying, (quartz and obsidian are two good choices), have self-lighting charcoal for the brazier (or cauldron), and write messages on pieces of paper for your loved ones who have passed over (one piece of paper for each individual you wish to contact).

The Altar

Cover the altar in a black or orange cloth. Decorate it with traditional Halloween touches, such as an iron cauldron, bats, owls, brooms, and skeletons. Add a pomegranate to represent the cycle of life-death-rebirth at one side of the brazier; place your messages to loved ones on the other. Put the black and white candles at opposite sides of the table's surface.

Invocation

Begin the ritual when it is totally dark outside. This invocation begins with a prayer that opens the way for the spirits of beloved friends and ancestors to join you: *"Lady and Lord, pull aside the veil; the edge of time where all things begin and end. Open a gateway to my loved ones that they may join me in this rite."*

Cast the circle starting in the west, the region where several cultures believe the afterlife abides.

WEST

I, _____ [give as much of your lineage as you know—for example, mine would be "Patricia, daughter of Ruth and Karl, daughter and son of Raymond and Elsie..."], *come into the circle of Water, a circle of might, to sing of my family on this holy night.*" Place a familial token on the western point to welcome those spirits.

NORTH

I come into the circle of Earth, the circle of peace, so wandering spirits may be released. Place a knife or pair of scissors here to symbolize the freeing of ties. (Some spirits linger in the Earth plane because they feel compelled to watch over loved ones.)

EAST

I come into the circle of Air, a circle of change. Let the old be transformed, by spirit rearranged. Leave an emblem here of what you plan to transform in the ritual using the black and white candles.

SOUTH

I come into the circle of Fire, a circle of song, as the light grows shorter, and night grows long. Extinguish a candle at this point of the circle to represent the season's darkness.

CENTER

I come into the circle of the Ancients, a circle of light, and welcome familial spirits, this All Souls' Night.

Light a central candle, any color you choose, to represent the Spirit's presence.

Meditation and Visualization

Hallows is a time for remembering, and for journeying into our own subconscious. This sojourn unlocks the keys for integrating our past, and handling the present more effectively. For this meditation, sit with the crystal you have chosen and close your eyes. Think of one person, now deceased, whom you would trust as a guide, and ask silently for his or her guidance.

Breathe deeply and slowly. Feel the energy of the crystal in your hand. For now, let it sit idly here, lending its insightful power to the meditation process. If it helps, lie on the floor with the crystal resting on your Third Eye while you meditate.

Envision all those friends and family members who have passed over in a circle around you, linking hands. Let their love become the magic sphere that holds you in this place between worlds. As you feel this protective, caring energy grow, the crystal will begin to get warm. When this happens, open your eyes and take the crystal in hand.

Think now of one question that has been nagging you. Direct that question into the crystal. Look at the surface of the stone, and let your gaze become naturally blurry. Watch for images to appear. You may see literal portraits, symbols, or clouds in response to your question. Portraits and symbols have to be interpreted by you. Generally bright or white clouds moving up or to the right are good omens, while those appearing dark, or moving down and to the left are negative portents.

After you receive your answer, whisper your thanks to the spirits who watched over you, and to the stone. Make notes of the experience in your ritual journal.

The Ritual

Stand before your altar, saying: *"I welcome the Old Ones, I offer hospitality to kindly guiding spirits in this sacred space. Those of you who chose to join me here, I beg a boon. Into these fires I place messages for people close to my heart."* Place the pieces of paper on which you've written your messages to departed loved ones into the cauldron of fire. *"Impart these words gently to* _____ [fill in with the names of the people you wish to contact]. *Carry the smoke of my love and memories with you into the next world when you return."* This is a good point in the ritual to look over old scrap books and revel in positive memories. Allow tears to flow freely, along with laughter as part of the circle of life.

Next, light the black candle, saying, *"Death is a part of life. Today* _____ [fill in with whatever you've chosen to release] *dies* within me. *This is not a loss, but a liberating change that I welcome and accept.*" If possible, dance the circle counterclockwise at this point to release negativity. Keep moving until you feel finished casting the shadows from your life.

Light the white candle, saying, "*From death to the old ways comes life anew. I light the candle of* _____ [fill in with a characteristic you hope to gain] *that it may always shine in my heart.*" Dance, or walk, the circle clockwise to draw positive energy, and bring light to the darkness.

Other Activities

If you can take a trip to the graves of family or friends later, it's traditional to leave soul cakes there as an offering to the spirits of the departed. At home, leave out sweet cream for the Fey so they don't cause mischief.

Some people hold a séance tonight, or attempt other forms of divination, such as pendulum work. If you hold a séance, please make sure that an experienced medium controls the attempt. There are many spirits wandering Earth, and you don't want to accidentally reach the wrong one!

Pendulum divination is actually fairly easy to try. You'll need a length of cotton or wool string that's as long as your elbow-to-fingertip measurement, plus a little extra. Thread a needle, wedding band, or other evenly weighted object onto this. Put the elbow of your strong hand on the table, with the pendulum hanging down from between your pointer finger and thumb. Steady the pendulum, then think of a yes or no question. Clockwise or up-and-down movement is a positive answer; counterclockwise or left-and-right movement indicates a negative answer.

Closing the Circle

Put away the tokens you've placed at each quarter point as you recite this dismissal. Note that the progression of the closing gives the attending spirits time to leave before the veil is closed again.

SOUTH
I release the circle of song,
the circle of Fire.
The way is opened by a cleansing pyre.

EAST
I release the circle of change,
the circle of Air.
The way is new, but the magic is there.

NORTH
I release the circle of peace,
the circle of Earth.
The way is fertile for spirit's rebirth.

WEST
I release the circle of Water,
the circle of might.
The way is ready; spirits, take flight!

CENTER
I release the circle of the Ancients,
the circle of light.
The way is closed, this holy night.

Closing Prayer (Optional)

> *Lady and Lord, I have released, sown, and reaped…now it is time*
> *to rest. Bring peace to my spirit, to all those souls here gathered, and*
> *to this place until we meet here again. So be it.*

Postritual Foods

Traditionally, animals enjoy the food first today, in thankfulness
for the gift of sustenance many of them offer. After that, try
cultural foods or favorite edibles of the departed people honored
in your ritual.

Don't let the leftover pumpkin go to waste; make pie or bread as a protective food. Also consider dark foods, such as rye or pumpernickel bread. Pork and apples are both customary foods for the dead, and beans are also a good choice—they grow counterclockwise!

10

Samhain Ritual

Preparations

Gather an apple, a pomegranate, and one pot of earth, containing three seeds of rue or lavender for each participant. Strew the sacred space with richly colored fall leaves, and mark the quarters with differently carved pumpkins that each bear an unlit candle.

The Altar

The apple, pomegranate, and pots of earth need to be on the altar's surface, if possible. Otherwise, leave the pots around the base of the table. Add any decorations suitable to autumn that you wish.

Invocation

Begin this invocation in the south and end in the west, going counterclockwise to mark the time of death. The candles in the pumpkins are ignited by the person reciting the quarter invocation.

SOUTH
The moon is bright, the Crone is old,
the body is lifeless, the bones so cold.

We all live and pay our dues
to die in ones, and threes, and twos.

EAST
Death, dance and play the harp,
piercing silence in the dark.
The Woman's old with withered limbs;
Death beckons her to dance with him.

NORTH
As she accepts the Dance of Death,
the Earth is cooled by ghostly breath
to lie in dormancy once more
to have her strength and life restored.

WEST
All ye spirits who walk the night,
hearken, hearken to my call.
I bid you in our circle join;
enter, enter, one and all!
Speak to us of things unknown;
lend your energies to this rite
to speed your journey we have joined
on this sacred Samhain night.

CENTER
O Mighty Pan of the Summerlands,
guardian of the beloved dead,
we pour forth love on those you keep safely
in your peaceful stead.
We bless those who have walked the path
that someday we as well shall rove.
We offer peace unto their souls
While resting in your arms below.

Meditation and Visualization

It is helpful to create a guided meditation whereby each person
can welcome the spirit of a deceased person (or even a pet) whom

they love to the circle. This is an opportunity for the participants to establish some closure in these relationships, so bring plenty of tissue.

The Ritual

The leader goes to the altar, holding up the pomegranate toward the sky and saying, *"Behold the fruit of life!"* The leader pierces the fruit with a ritual dagger and continues, *"Whose seeds lie in the dormancy of death. We taste the seeds of death."* The leader eats of the fruit, then passes it around the circle. Each participant takes one seed and eats it.

The leader now takes the apple and holds it up, saying, *"Behold the fruit of wisdom, the fruit of death."* He or she cuts this crosswise so the inner pentagram formed by the seeds can be seen and continues, *"Whose symbolism rewards us with life eternal—the fivefold star of rebirth! We taste the fruit of rebirth."* The leader eats a small slice and gives one to each participant, as with the pomegranate.

After this the leader presents each person with a pot of soil, explaining that it represents the time of dormancy and potential. This is a time when all should reevaluate their lives, and plant three values (the seeds) they wish to cultivate. Once everyone has channeled his or her hopes into the pots, each person holds the pot to the sky, saying thrice:

> *The sun is conceived in darkness, cold;*
> *in the shadow of death, life unfolds;*
> *a shred of light begins to burn;*
> *from death comes life, the circle turns.*

Other Activities

At some point in the ritual, those who wish to may use divination tools to speak with the spirits assembled. People should take notes of their experiences and any messages received.

Closing the Circle

Banishing begins in the western quarter and continues clockwise to symbolize hope and fulfillment:

Blessings upon thee, wondrous spirits of Summerland. We humbly thank you for joining in celebrations this sacred night. We beseech thee, Pan, guardian of the dead, embrace once again those souls in your keeping, that even the lost and wandering find their way to peace. Let them stay with you until they are refreshed and reborn in perfect love. We bid thee a fond farewell. So mote it be!

11

Winter Solstice: December 22

This is one of my favorite celebrations. At this time of year, every corner of our Victorian home shimmers with holiday decorations. Pinecones hang from windows as a symbol of rebirth, nuts adorn tables for prosperity, shiny ornaments repel negativity, and the Yule tree fills the air with the fresh, healthy aroma of pine.

The alternative name for this day, Yule, comes from a Gaelic word meaning "wheel," most likely alluding to the solar wheel turning again. In earlier times, Winter Solstice often included feasts for various greater gods such as Odin and Osiris, who also have strong connections with the sun. This is not surprising: this day marks the end of the solar year, when the sun's height on the horizon reaches its lowest point, then grows again.

Symbolically this signals the Crone goddess stirring in the womb of Earth, bringing hope to winter's cold. She will be resurrected in spring as a young woman, and dance with the fertile Earth.

Preparations

If it's physically feasible, fast and pray for three days beforehand. This allows you to enter the new year's cycle purified in body and

spirit. Also consider a ritual bath with cinnamon, mint, and rose petals to improve psychic awareness.

Decorate the sacred space with gold and silver spheres to represent the returning sun, and wreaths to symbolize the turning Wheel. Have oak shavings ready as a base for your incense. Add any other personally meaningful herbs to this mixture and start burning it before the invocation to help prepare the sacred space. Finally, put your sun candle from earlier in the year at the southern point of the circle.

The Altar

Cover the table with a pale green cloth—the color of early sprouts, which represent continuance. Add red berries for life's blood; holly; ivy; and pine branches as a symbol of longevity. The pine also welcomes sylvan spirits to your circle.

Have a Yule log at the center point, placing there your God and Goddess candles. Always keep part of the candles or the log itself for future years; this brings good luck, life, health, and providence.

Invocation

Light the Goddess candle in the Yule log, then move to the northern point of your circle. This is the quarter traditionally ascribed to the season of winter.

NORTH
Ancient Mother, I look for your opulence, but tonight naught but barren trees decorate the land. In this restful moment, let my spirit find healing.

EAST
Ancient Brother, I listen for your winds, but tonight they are still. In this quiet darkness, help me find inspiration.

SOUTH
Ancient Father, I look for your fires, but tonight the embers only begin to glow more brightly. May this gentle warmth temper my spirit.

WEST

Ancient Sister, I seek your glistening tears, but tonight they are frozen. Beneath this cool blanket, let my emotions find stability.

CENTER

Ancient Ones, I seek your face, but tonight darkness surrounds. Help me find your spark within to guide my path.

Meditation and Visualization

Winter Solstice is an excellent time to undergo a vision quest to find your magical name, a totem animal, a mantra, or other empowering insights. This meditation is meant to accent that quest by opening your awareness to the power within and without all things.

Begin in a standing position. Center yourself and breathe deeply. Slowly take off your mundane clothes, likewise removing the "world" with each. Wrap a blanket around yourself for warmth, but remain naked for the meditation. You need no trappings to discover personal power.

Sit and close your eyes. Let any remaining tension drain away, then begin listening to the sound of silence. Smell the aromas of oak and herb. Feel the latent energy of everything around you and the magic you've placed there. Know it as your own.

Listen to your breath and your heartbeat. Sense the pulse and ebb within as the same energy without. Listen closely; does it whisper a message to you? Does it whisper a name? Do you hear the cry of an animal? Do you hear words that fill you with energy? Linger in this place between Earth and stars until you receive a message. Then return to normal levels of awareness, and write of the experience in your journal.

The Ritual

Turn toward the northern part of your circle. Think of things that you want to banish, such as bad habits. Say: *"I call to the darkness.*

Come embrace my _____ [fill in with your negative characteristics]. *Take them to yourself. I release them. As the sun climbs in the sky, take these things with you in retreat, never to return to me again."*

Turn to the south of the circle, light the sun candle, and repeat this chant. Let it naturally grow to fill the entire space with positive vibrations:

> *Strong sun, returning sun;*
> *the light burns as the Wheel turns*
> *Strong sun, returning sun;*
> *the shadows fade; by magic bade*
> *strong sun, returning sun;*
> *the shadows flee, the magic is free!*

Return to the altar now and light the God candle, using the Goddess candle as a fire source (symbolic of the womb).

Sun Father, your journey has left you weary. May this light give you strength to reach toward the heavens again with warmth and brilliance.

After so saying, go through your home and light all its candles, lamps, flashlights, or decorative lights to represent the sun's return.

Other Activities

Make symbolic decorations for the tree. The traditional pastime of stringing popcorn and cranberries can symbolize continued providence, for example. Or bundle scraps of yellow cloth with brightly colored ribbons, tying in wishes as you go.

Another customary activity in rural communities is the blessing of fruit-bearing trees. If you don't have a fruit tree nearby, use any indoor plant as a substitute. Sprinkle it with wassail mixed with the ash from your incense. This helps manifest a productive year.

Finally, make predictions for the coming year based on the weather. Folklore says a white Christmas brings prosperity, while a green one precedes a bad year for crops; when the sun shines through fruit trees on the Winter Solstice, it foreshadows abundance.

Closing the Circle

WEST
Spirit of the West, thank you for cleansing body, mind, and spirit. As you go from this place, likewise purify Earth.

SOUTH
Spirit of the South, thank you for this warmth of body, mind, and spirit. As you go from this place, likewise generate love on Earth.

EAST
Spirit of the East, thank you for this stillness of body, mind, and spirit. As you go from this place, likewise bring peace to Earth.

NORTH
Spirit of the North, thank you for healing me in body, mind, and spirit. As you go from this place, likewise heal Earth.

CENTER
Ancient Ones, thank you for the turning Wheel that enlightens body, mind, and spirit. As you go from this place, likewise edify Earth.

Postritual Foods

Go with your traditional holiday foods, which for me include many that have solar symbolism. Cookies are round like the sun, eggnog is golden and fertile, gingerbread is hot and spicy, and fruitcake bears red and orange highlights. As a side, try a little flaming brandy to warm you up!

PART III

Magic in the Moon

I [the moon] am the daughter of Earth and Water
and the nursling of the sky;
I pass through the pores of the ocean and shores
I change, but I cannot die.

—Percy Bysshe Shelley

The ancients believed that Witches received power from the moon. This idea may have started in Greece, where Hecate (the goddess of the Underworld and the moon) was the patroness of Witches. Whatever the reason, while the Wiccan Wheel commemorates the movement of the sun, and the seasons of Earth, the moon also figures predominantly into magical rites.

For one thing, many spells and charms include lunar timing as part of their instructions, according to either the moon's phase or its placement among the stars. Second, Esbats, which come between the Sabbats previously covered, are rituals that honor the moon's cycles and symbolism. The most frequently observed Esbats are those of the Full Moon and Dark Moon.

As the moon waxes, it represents the Maiden brimming with potential. Wiccans use this phase of the moon to accent spells and rituals for growth, opportunity, cultivating skills or attributes, and improved productivity. As it reaches fullness, it is the Mother—the giver of life and creative power. This phase is suited to magic for accomplishment, completing projects, personal development, and both literal and figurative fertility.

In waning, the moon becomes the Crone, an astute guide to the great mysteries. Throughout this phase the moon slowly shrinks to darkness—a symbolic three-day death—only to be reborn again. Magic during this phase focuses on banishing our shadows, protection, and manifesting wisdom and maturity.

Besides this basic symbolism, each month's moons—both full and dark—were named by the ancients. These names can give your lunar observations throughout the year a unique focus, if you so choose. Beginning in January, the full Wolf Moon's theme is how to tenaciously search out what we need. The dark Quiet Moon reveals the value of silence and contemplation.

Come February, the Storm Moon turns our attention onto the light around that helps guide us through difficult times. The dark Hunger Moon gives us pause to be grateful for what we have, and for Earth's providence. In March, the full Plow Moon gives us illumination with which to cultivate our spirits, and the dark Seed Moon provides the time to plant the attributes necessary to a growing soul. Other names to consider for focal points in your lunar observation include:

Month	Full Moon	Dark Moon
April	Budding Moon (growth)	Planting Moon (sowing)
May	Mother's Moon (Goddess)	Ninth Moon (fulfillment)
June	Mead Moon (grace)	Strawberry Moon (abundance)
July	Claiming Moon (affirmation)	Blessing Moon (Divine favor)
August	Dispute Moon (ending anger)	Harvest Moon (reaping rewards)
September	Wine Moon (celebration)	Singing Moon (sounds and silences)
October	Blood Moon (life's energy)	Falling Leaf Moon (cycles)
November	Morning Moon (beginnings)	Dead Moon (banishing)
December	Oak Moon (Nature's lessons)	Snow Moon (rest)

12

Full Moon Ritual

"Lady of the Night, be my guide. Lady of the Moon, stand by my side."
I recite these words sometimes when standing outside beneath the
full moon. As the silver light pours down, I am reminded that my
spirit, like the moon, is always changing and growing. This indeed
is the essence of magic.

The full moon reflects the Mother, whose maturity and
nurturing inspires the best in us, her children. It is a night for
fulfillment and manifestation—a time to gather what we sow, to
take responsibility, and to respectfully weave the power within us
without fear.

Preparations

Prepare a ritual bath with feminine, lunar, or water herbs to honor
the moon's fullness. Suggestions include jasmine or mint (lunar),
chamomile or lily (water), and rose or vanilla (feminine).

Find a large bowl into which you can place your moon candle
so it's surrounded by water. Affix the candle to the center of the
bowl using some melted wax, then add water until it's three-
quarters full. Pour a little pearly white dishwashing soap on the
surface of this so it looks like a full moon!

Besides these preparations, you will also need two white or silver candles, a round mirror, and a white or blue cloth. If possible, choose ritual clothing that is white or silver in color.

The Altar

Cover the altar with the cloth. A little silver tinsel left over from Yule is a nice touch; when illuminated by candles, it looks much like moonlight. To the right and left of the altar, place the white or silver candles to represent the Divine. The round mirror (the moon) goes at the center, with the moon candle behind it.

Invocation

EAST
Celestial Winds, come dance and sing;
with you, airs of inspiration bring.
Full and rich, to my heart,
all your wisdom pray impart.

SOUTH
Cosmic Fires, come dance and sing;
with you, sparks of cleansing bring.
Full and rich, to my heart,
all your strength pray impart.

WEST
Astral Waters, come dance and sing;
with you, waves of insight bring.
Full and rich, to my heart,
all your creativity pray impart.

NORTH
Stellar Earth, come dance and sing;
with you, soils of flowering bring.
Full and rich, to my heart,
all your rooting pray impart.

CENTER
Shining Spirit, come dance and sing;
with you, the magic of harmony bring.
Full and rich, to my heart,
all your power pray impart.

Meditation and Visualization

Sit down where you are and breathe deeply. There is no need to rush; now is a time of softness, of quiet knowing. See yourself in your mind's eye as you sit. Above you is a smiling moon, in full glory.

As you look upon the lunar sphere, you see that the light is alive. It dances, and sings a special song. It jumps from the surface like a fire and travels downward to embrace you. The touch is cool, yet warm.

It reaches beyond your skin and saturates every pore, every cell—you are the moonlight; you are the shadow of a star. There is no body now to hold you back. Let your spirit fly with the moon wherever it needs to go. Make notes about this experience afterward in your ritual journal.

The Ritual

The actual ritual for a full moon will depend greatly on the focus you chose. One thing I do recommend, however, is including a Moon Charge shortly after your invocation. An example of a Full Moon Charge begins by lighting a long-handled match and holding it to the sky, saying:

> *As she shines fully in the sky,*
> *the Lady shines in my heart, and in my home.*

Next, light the moon candle you've created, saying:

Mother Moon, welcome!
Mother Moon, come!
Your tides of power bring fulfillment,
and your beams bear the realization of change.

After this, look to the surface of the water where the moon candle sits. Take a deep, cleansing breath and say:

Tides that sway and tides that flow;
as above, so below;
The moon once small, now fully seen
in this bowl, my future bring.

See what movement, shapes, or images appear in the light that dances on the water. Clockwise movement portends good things to come in the next month. Counterclockwise swirling represents the need for caution. Take mental note of any shapes and images that strike you with additional insight. For example, clockwise movement forming a heart would indicate a love interest making itself known before the next full moon.

Other Activities

If you need improved finances, turn your wallet or purse by the light of a waxing crescent moon three times to draw money to you. Make sure you first spy the full moon when outdoors. This brings luck.

To dream true, go out on the first night of a full moon and whisper your desire for a visionary dream to the Lady. (This procedure is especially effective when you wish to see a future mate.) Return inside in silence, and go directly to bed. Keep a notebook handy so that you can record your dreams upon waking.

Take your moon mirror outside on the second night of the full moon and let the light shine upon it. Then use that mirror for scrying the future. Finally, sow magical herbs during the waxing-to-full moon cycle to improve their heartiness and power.

Closing the Circle

NORTH
Stellar Earth, your blossoms close,
but in my heart their fragrance grows.

WEST
Astral Waters, your waves subside
into my heart, there to reside.

SOUTH
Cosmic Fires, your sparks wane,
but in my heart they live again.

EAST
Celestial Winds, your airs fade,
but carry the magic, as I bade.

CENTER
Shining Spirit, your song still sings,
and with it now the magic brings!

Postritual Foods

Make white moon cakes, or enjoy other white foods such as cauliflower, pita, milk, and cucumbers. Also consider seafood, since the ocean is so strongly connected to the lunar cycle.

13

Dark Moon Ritual

The sky is filled with stars, piercing the black veil like silver turrets topping an invisible castle. The moon is nowhere to be found; it hides in the dark sea awaiting rebirth. Herein the dark moon becomes a representation of deep mysteries—that which is, but isn't—things that exist, but cannot be seen.

For Wiccans, the dark moon is a time of reflection on our own shadows. As the moon wanes we banish negativity, then rest in the darkness, the womb of night also awaiting our rebirth. Then as we see the first glimmer of a sliver of waxing moon, our hearts ignite with magic.

Preparations

Have as little light for this ritual as possible. The darkness prevails. A nice decorative touch indoors is to place glow-in-the-dark stars on the ceiling.

Take a ritual bath in restful, contemplative herbs, then don a black robe upon which silver stars are painted. Take out your moon candle and mirror, a dark cloth, and one candle to represent the Divine.

The Altar

Cover the altar with the black cloth, then sprinkle its surface with glitter. When touched by candlelight, the effect is of stars. Have the moon candle lit when you come into the sacred space.

Invocation

Some people may wish to invoke the Quarters counterclockwise for decrease and banishing, depending on the focus of your personal ritual.

EAST
Quiet Winds, hushed and calm, be alert, but gentle in this eastern quarter of creation and the magic circle, protecting it from all dangers.

SOUTH
Muted Embers, warm and welcoming, be alert, but faint in this southern quarter of creation and the magic circle, protecting it from all dangers.

WEST
Soft rains, fertile and filling, be alert, but hushed in this western quarter of creation and the magic circle, protecting it from all dangers.

NORTH
Rich Earth, cool and nurturing, be alert, but silent in this northern quarter of creation and the magic circle, protecting it from all dangers.

CENTER
Living Spirit, guiding and empowering, be alert, and bind the energy of creation in this magic circle, protecting it from all dangers.

From the burning moon candle, light the candle that you've chosen to represent the Divine's presence here.

Meditation and Visualization

Sit where you are, or lie down. Consider the sounds of silence; the still small lights that flicker in the darkness. In the darkness of your own spirit, light always resides, just like the stars in the sky without the moon. Explore this inner dimension, and find those sparks. There are many.

Each light within your spirit's sky represents a positive attribute that you've developed until it shines without fear through the darkness. Name them as they appear, quietly, one by one. Reclaim all attributes as your night lights—guidelines with which to traverse any darkness you come upon.

Make notes of the experience in your journal.

The Ritual

Stand in front of the altar, taking the dark cloth in hand, saying: "She shines no more in the sky. The Lady rests, but in my heart, and mind, and soul, the light remains." Cover the moon mirror. "This circle is the world between worlds, where all things are possible—Luna is missing. She hides. Like Jonah in the belly of the whale, the moon has been swallowed into the womb of space." Blow out the moon candle.

Raise your athame, wand, or hand toward the sky, saying:

Dark Moon hail!
Crone Moon hail!
In this moment of darkness and quiet
let me discover clarity, truth—
and the light of my own spirit.

Other Activities

If you happen to be a gardener, this is an excellent time to till and weed, as well as planting any below-ground vegetables such as radishes, potatoes, or carrots.

Anyone who follows the Egyptian god Horus would do well to honor him in some manner in the sacred space. According to legend, the dark moon and the full moon are this god's eyes.

Finally, this is an excellent night to pursue visionary dreams.

Drink a tea of rose and jasmine during your ritual, and pour the rest out to the dark moon, asking for its guidance while you sleep. After the ritual go right to bed, keeping your journal handy.

Closing the Circle

Dismissal of this ritual begins in the north, the region of darkness:

NORTH
Guardians of the North, I thank you for the gentle soils in which my spirit grows. Go from this place in peace.

WEST
Guardians of the West, I thank you for the soothing waters that enrich my soul. Go from this place in peace.

SOUTH
Guardians of the South, I thank you for the warm fires that always burn within me. Go from this place in peace.

EAST
Guardians of the East, I thank you for the soft breezes of magic that motivate me. Go from this place in peace.

CENTER
Great Spirit, I thank you for the sparks of light and truth that you placed within, granting guidance even in the darkness. Go from this place in peace.

Postritual Foods

Try any dark-colored foods such as rye or pumpernickel bread, chocolate cake, potatoes with the skin on, and the like.

14

New Moon (First Quarter) Ritual

The first quarter moon represents both endings and beginnings. The old is gone into the stellar sea with the dark moon. The new arrives with a sliver of hopeful light appearing on the horizon. Wiccans use this symbolism for empowering new projects, starting groups, and personal development.

This particular First Quarter Ritual is intended for a study group; it's used to establish a good foundation for rapport with those involved. It is shared here with thanks to David Ledwin for the contribution.

For those of you who work alone, I suggest adapting this ritual's symbolism for times when you're embarking on a course of personal study, a new job for which you need to develop specific skills, and the like. Just adjust the candle's color and your incense to match the intentions of the magic.

Preparations

Have elementally colored candles at the circle's quarter points (unlit). Sprinkle the ritual space with dulse, orris root, and copal for cleansing, and improved awareness. All participants will also need to choose one candle to represent their presence in the sacred space, anoint it with a personal oil, and then put it on the altar in a candleholder.

The Altar

Use a silvery blue altar cloth with a white and black candle, an athame, a bowl of water, a bowl of salt, a goblet of wine, cakes, and censer with incense of your choosing. The individual candles should be arranged in a circle to represent unity of mind and purpose.

Invocation

Light the candles at the quarter points while reciting each part of the invocation:

NORTH
Protectors of the Forest and Its People,
we/I call to you.
O enrichers of life and revelry,
be welcome.

EAST
Singers of the Songs of the Wind and the Birds,
we/I call to you.
In thoughtfulness, and with dedicated spirit,
welcome.

SOUTH
Leapers of Fire and Faith, and of blazing stars,
we/I call to you.
Come forth from the darting flames
and be welcome.

WEST
Waters of Mirth and Merriment, and of Neptune's
gale, we/I call to you.

Liberate your mist and waves of grace
and be welcome in this place.

Meditation and Visualization

Have everyone in the group hold hands around the circle and close their eyes. Someone should read this meditation slowly, giving everyone present time to integrate the energies.

See a silvery moon shining in the center of your being. It is just beginning to grow from out of the darkness. Focus on this energy, this power, and let it grow within you. Slowly, perceptibly, it fills every corner of your being and pours outward to the center of this circle. Here, it dances and mingles with the spirits of all those gathered... bringing balance, harmony, tolerance...perfect love...perfect trust. Let this energy swirl and combine, then burst outward in all directions, purifying everything in its path. Breathe of this cleansing energy, and let it relax you. Continue breathing of the light until you are comfortable in its glow, then open your eyes.

If you're working alone, you can use the visualization by changing the mention of "spirits" to "elemental powers." In this case, consider pretaping the guided visualization for yourself so you can listen to it while meditating.

The Ritual

One by one, all participants come forward, light their personal candles, and state their names. They also mention any personal goals they have in joining the group. When everyone is done, a discussion of the group, its purpose and goals, follows within the equality and protection of the circle.

Afterward the cake and wine are blessed by a chosen person, saying: *"Lord and Lady, Powers of Sea and Sky, we ask your blessing upon these cakes and this drink. Let the sharing of this cup bring unity, accord, and peace."* Each person takes a drink and passes the cup to the person on the right. As the cup is passed, each says, *"Welcome and blessed be."*

After this, chant the words to a song used in many Wiccan circles:

> *We are a circle*
> *within a circle*
> *with no beginning, and never ending.*

Any remaining cakes and wine should be left as offerings to the spirits and Nature.

Other Activities

Look at the crescent moon over your right shoulder to bring luck. Sow your aboveground crops now, and possibly your magical herbs so they will grow full with power, like the moon grows in the sky. Put yarrow sprigs on the altar during the ritual, then take them home and put the herb under your pillow to have prophetic dreams.

To increase your finances by the next first quarter moon, put nine silver coins on the altar to gather energy during the ritual. Make sure they rest beneath the light of the waxing moon every night for seven nights after this, absorbing its energy. Carry these in a white or silver pouch with you until money manifests, then give the coins to a good cause.

Closing the Circle

WEST
Crashing Waves of Joy,
thank you for joining us with waves of mirth.
Hail and farewell.

SOUTH
Keepers of the Cauldron of Faith and Fire,
thank you for joining us in the warmth of unity.
Hail and farewell.

EAST
Singers of the Wind, in whom magic takes flight,
thank you for joining us with blustery delight.
Hail and farewell.

NORTH
Protectors of the Forest,
thank you for joining us in spirit and sanctity.
Hail and farewell.

CENTER
We have gathered together; we are one.
The circle is open, but not broken.
Merry meet, merry part, and merry meet again.
So mote it be!

Postritual Foods

In the spirit of sharing, enjoy a potluck feast.

PART IV

Personal Observances

*The holiest of all holidays are those
kept by ourselves in silence and apart,
the secret anniversaries of the heart,
when the full tide of feeling overflows.*

—Henry Wadsworth Longfellow

The Wiccan Wheel of the Seasons revolves around the axis of universal rhythms, the seasons, the sun, and the moon. The center of this axis, however, is the individual—the soul questing for enlightenment and understanding. Consequently, there are other Wiccan ceremonies throughout the year to commemorate all that it means to be human—our joys, our sorrows, our goals, and our successes.

While some rituals have been detailed in various Wiccan traditions for these types of observances, most that I've seen are highly personalized and creative, which seems best. Each individual is a wholly unique being, and the rituals that engender profound meaning and significance for the participants must be likewise unique. So personalizing ritual becomes the key for intimate, purposeful magic that helps us integrate our life experiences.

Consider the rituals in this section as a rough sketch from which you can draft your own celebrations. Add to them as much personal vision as possible, including symbols, songs, poems, clothing, edibles, and such that suit the moment. Trust in your heart as the best guide to designing empowering, memorable rituals that will bless everyone present.

15

Initiation

When you follow the Wiccan Path, one of the first, and most important, steps is that of initiation. This is a time when a group welcomes a new member who has chosen to study and grow with that group. In part 1 of this book, I outlined a personal dedication for people who do not have access to Wiccan groups, or who choose to work alone. This ritual is the companion piece for group use, contributed in part by David Ledwin.

Consider holding this ritual during the time of a new moon, to represent a new cycle. The themes of this ritual are beginnings, community, spirituality, and dedication.

Preparations

For the ritual you will need a brazier or fireproof container, self-lighting charcoal, red wine, a goblet, an athame or wand, a feather, anointing oils, and sage. It's also nice to have a new ritual robe for the initiate, provided by either the newcomer or the group. Alternatively, prepare some type of crystal, charged by each member of the group, to give as a welcoming gift to the initiate during the ritual.

Before the rite, the initiate should be somewhere quiet where he or she can meditate alone. Also, set up a curtain through which the initiate can enter the sacred space. This curtain marks the passage from the old life into the new, from the mundane realms into magic.

The Altar

Cover the altar with any colored cloth desired. For example, green is a nice choice for beginnings and growth. Place the brazier (or fireproof container) at one side of the circle with the sage and the feather. Put the cup filled with red wine at the other side.

Invocation

This invocation takes the form of a prayer, during which the leader of the group walks the circle with the burning sage. Use the feather to fan the smoke outward for protection:

Lady of the Moon, God of the Rising Sun,
protectors all, we invoke your presence to witness this rite.
Let the powers of Air and Fire, Water and Earth swirl 'round,
safeguarding this sacred space and empowering it with magic.
As your servants, we come in unity.
Give us the wisdom and strength,
the perfect love and trust to welcome a new member among us.
So be it.

Meditation and Visualization

This guided meditation is for the group to perform before the initiate comes in. One person recites the visualization, or a tape recording can be used so everyone can participate. Quiet music seems to enhance the effectiveness of guided meditations, so see if you can find an appropriate tape or CD.

See the sparkling shimmer of magic swirling around you. It is part of you, part of each of us. We are one in the magic; one bright sphere of light that surrounds this room. Breathe of the light, let it fill you, hold you, and heal you [pause].

Watch the magic dance from person to person; see it play in their auras, then dance on, until each of us waltzes in power from the others here gathered....Yet someone is missing....The dance lulls without all its partners. Prepare your heart to welcome that partner [pause].

Visualize love as a warm pink light and direct it toward the curtain through which our new member shall soon pass [pause]. *Leave the light of your love here, the light of unity, then slowly return to normal awareness. When you feel ready, open your eyes.*

The Ritual

A sponsor from the group goes to get the initiate. As the initiate passes through the curtain, the sponsor hands him or her the magical robe, saying, *"You walk now in a place between worlds, time without time. Leave the mundane behind you, and don the mantle of magic as you enter the sacred space."* The initiate puts on the robe and is guided to the leader, who will use the feather to smudge the initiate's aura with sage smoke. The leader also makes the symbol of a pentagram over the initiate's Third Eye using that person's athame or wand, then gives it to the initiate, saying, *"Use this tool wisely and responsibly. Let it guide you through this circle to the guardians to be welcome."* The initiate places the tool in his or her belt sheath.

The sponsor takes the initiate to each quarter of the circle, starting in the east, the point of beginnings. The initiate stands before the point while the sponsor says, *"Guardians of the Outer Realms, watch over this person on the path he/she begins today. Guide him/her in all things that word and deed both bear the Air* [change Air to Fire, Water, or Loam, depending on the quarter in which you stand] *of magic."* If possible, have some appropriate anointing oils at each quarter mark—patchouli for Earth, lavender for Air, rosemary for Fire, and rose for Water. Dab a bit of this on the initiate's heart chakra and each palm.

After completing the salute to the last quarter, the initiate says: "*I give my hands and heart in working magic for the greatest good.*" The sponsor says, "*the Winds [Flames, Waves, or Seeds] have witnessed your promise and convey it through the web of all things from which we receive and direct our magic.*"

The initiate moves to the center of the circle where the leader of the group hands him or her a goblet. "*This is the cup of unity. By drinking of it you make a commitment to all here gathered to protect, nurture, and energize our magic together in the spirit of perfect love and trust. Do you accept this charge?*"

The initiate responds, "*I do so freely.*"

The leader continues, "*Then I ask you by what name you choose to be called in this sacred space. Whisper it now to my ear.*" The initiate tells the leader the chosen magical name. The leader then walks with the initiate around the circle clockwise, introducing him or her by this new name to each person present. As the two of them walk, the members of the circle also partake of the cup.

Other Activities

During this last circuit of introductions, a crystal or other gift for the initiate might be passed. As each person holds it, he or she charges it with a wish for the initiate. Examples include, "*May this crystal bring you peace*" and "*May this crystal bear our united energies.*"

Closing the Circle

The remainder of the cup is poured out by way of an offering as the leader says:

Old Ones, Ancestors, God and Goddess all,
I pour this with a thankful heart,
for today we have a new brother/sister.
May each of us be an example
of the power, promise, and potential in magic.

As we each go from this place,
watch over us, and particularly _____ [initiate's magic name]
until we meet again.
The circle is open, but never broken.
Hail and farewell.
All coven members repeat: *"Hail and farewell!"*

Postritual Foods

It's nice to let the initiate make requests for favored edibles.

16

Adulthood

Turn turn, turn my wheel. 'Tis nature's plan that a child should grow into a man.

—Henry Longsworth

Among both Wiccans and Pagans, a Coming of Age Ritual acknowledges the physical maturity that time brings. Exactly when this ritual takes place depends on your outlook. For young girls, it might happen after their first menstruation. Yet this, in itself, does not indicate a readiness for adulthood in our complex world. Instead, I recommend holding a Coming of Age Ritual when a child shows signs of making mature decisions and taking responsibility for his or her life.

Obviously, the Rite of Womanhood and the Rite of Manhood need to have distinct differences. Nonetheless, there are some similarities between the two that can be used to create a generic ritual construct. For the purpose of brevity, I have chosen to create a single ritual construct, noting some ideas for variations between the man's and woman's rites so that you can adapt it accordingly. Consider holding the rite during the time of a full moon to represent maturity. The themes of this ritual are new responsibility, growth, and potential.

Preparations

Prior to the ritual, the child should be secluded with other members of the same sex for a full day. This creates an excellent opportunity to discuss sexual matters, and the changing roles of men and women in today's society. The youth should be encouraged to ask questions and contribute freely to the discourse.

Additionally, during this time the child needs to choose a new name—a magical name that will indicate full membership in the circle. This name should reflect all that they are, and all that they wish to become. The reason for the name is important, but have the youth keep this to him- or herself until the appropriate time during the ritual.

Parents or guardians should prepare for the ritual by getting the child a gift, magical or mundane, that reflects the child's adult status. A good magical choice is the gift of an athame. A girl might also receive a lunar stone to honor her moon cycle, and a boy receive both condoms and something made of gold, an emblem of the sun and masculinity.

All participants should gather together pictures of the child at different ages. These will be used to decorate the sacred space. Finally, if the child so chooses, he or she can get a haircut. In many religious traditions, the cutting of hair marks a sacred calling and commitment to the Divine. The Rite of Adulthood is no less sacred, for a child is about to claim his or her power.

The Altar

For the girl's ritual, use Goddess statuettes, round crystals, a plethora of white flowers, and sweet-smelling incense. Have a bowl of rose water for aspurging.

For the boy's ritual, use God statuettes, crystal points, tree branches with leaves still attached, and anything that has a woody aroma. Have a bowl of water with patchouli oil mingled in for aspurging.

Set up pictures of the child in younger years at one side of the room, where the child will enter the circle. A current picture is on the other side, perhaps with a new robe or change of clothing and the parents' gifts.

Invocation

Before the invocation, a young girl crawls into the sacred space from between the women's legs, past the pictures of her youth. The young man might be carried by other men from a similar location. Both actions symbolize the baby, who does not walk independently. The child then takes a place in the center of the circle.

For women, the invocation focuses on the feminine element and the Goddess, while men focus on the God. A sample of each is given here. During either, the leader of the ritual should walk the circle with scented water in women's rites, and burning incense in men's rites. This marks the area with the appropriate energy.

GODDESS INVOCATION

Lady from whom we are born
and to whom we return,
we call to you for your presence.
Breathe on us with the wind of inspiration (east),
ignite in us the fires of womanhood (south),
water us with the rain of nurturing (west),
and ground us in your womb (north).
In this sacred space we are all sisters
of one magic, of one blood.

GOD INVOCATION

Lord of our beginnings
and to whom we shall return,
we call to you for your presence.

Breathe on us with the winds of conscious (east),
ignite in us the fires of manhood (south),
water us with waves of strength (west),
and ground us with roots of power (north),
In this sacred space we are all brothers
of one magic, of one seed.

Meditation and Visualization

Everyone sits in a circle holding hands around the youth, who sits in the center. The leader begins a guided mediation.

Breathe deeply and easily. Feel your connection to the people around you...not just the physical connection, but the bonds of woman/manhood. Visualize our unity as a silver/gold light that encompasses all here present. It glows with the warmth of our sisterhood/brotherhood. [The leader should direct everyone to drop hands, and turn their palms inward toward the youth.]

Gather the silver/golden light from around and above you. Let it saturate every cell of your being, then direct it to the center of the circle. Give of your radiance to this new woman/man, that it may empower her/his journey into adulthood. [The leader should wait until he or she senses everyone has completed this part.] *Open your eyes and breathe normally. Stand and greet your fellow.* [Everyone will give the youth a hug, then return to a spot in the circle.]

The Ritual

The leader faces the youth. *"Welcome _____ [name]. I bless you in the name of the God/Goddess as an adult member of this gathering. As this patchouli/rose water rushes through your aura, it bears away the child you once were, and empowers the man/woman you are becoming."* The leader now touches the youth's forehead with the water. *"Open your mind to mature thoughts. Open your mouth to learning words of wisdom* [touches the water to the youth's lips].

Open your heart [touches the heart chakra] *to giving and receiving love.*

"*Those here gathered have brought gifts to commemorate this day.*" All present now in turn give their gifts and explain the significance of the item to the recipient.

"*To mark this day you have chosen a new name,*" the leader continues. "*By what will you be called in this circle?*" The youth answers with the magical name.

"_____, *we welcome you as a brother/sister of this coven, and charge you to gather with us in perfect love and perfect trust. So be it.*"

Other Activities

A youth who has a special talent, such as music or writing poetry, might share this now with something suited to the moment. Additionally, the youth could be encouraged to speak of personal hopes and desires with regard to magical training from this point forward.

Closing the Circle

The youth should close the circle, because he or she is now considered an adult member of the group. This will give a sense of integration and closure.

Goddess Dismissal

Lady, I thank you for your blessings this day
and for guiding me safely into womanhood.
I know this is but the first step on a much longer path;
let your insight, gentle power, and beauty within me grow.
Farewell Brother Air, Father Fire, Sister Sea, Mother Earth.
As we leave from this place, watch over me
and all those here gathered
until we meet again beneath your loving gaze.
All coven members repeat: "*Farewell. Farewell.*"

GOD DISMISSAL

Lord, I thank you for your blessings this day
and for guiding me safely into manhood.
I know this is but the first step on a much longer path;
let your strength, courage, and leadership within me grow.
Farewell Brother Air, Father Fire, Sister Sea, Mother Earth.
As we leave from this place, watch over me
and all those here gathered
until we meet again beneath your golden gaze.
All coven members repeat: *"Farewell. Farewell."*

Postritual Foods

Things that a child would not normally be allowed to have before reaching adult status, such as coffee or beer, are one possibility. Otherwise, let the youth make requests for favored foods.

17

Marriage Ritual

Perhaps one of the most transformational experiences of any person's life is getting married. Two souls unite into a oneness of heart. In Wicca, this unity may be celebrated by either a Wedding or a Handfasting. The only difference between the two is that a Handfasting does not have to be legally binding. Instead, it acts as an agreement between two people to live in the bonds of love for a specific duration of time, after which both are free to stay or move on. In contemporary terms, it's like "living together."

For those trying to put together a Wiccan Wedding, I strongly suggest finding a minister with whom you can construct your celebration from the ground up. Some ministers will not work with a format outside their personal tradition; others will help you create something totally personal. The difference changes the format and feeling of the ritual tremendously.

Two rituals are presented here as helpmates to this process. The first comes with thanks to Jenny and Steven Sojka, whose medieval-style Wedding I performed in August 1997. The second is a Handfasting adapted from a ritual created by David Ledwin. Note that due to the uniqueness of Weddings, the pattern of the ritual is slightly different than the majority of rites covered in this book. Consider holding either the Wedding or the Handfasting during the time of a waxing moon to represent continued growth of the relationship into fullness.

Preparations

Create a sacred space *before* the actual ritual, using natural stones to mark the four quarters. This is especially important at Weddings in which the family is not Wiccan. It makes everyone more comfortable.

Items needed for the ritual itself include two candles to represent the bride and groom, a union candle, a cup with juice, a cauldron with charcoal, sweet bread, a sword or dagger, long matches, elemental tokens (a stone, seashell, match, and powdered incense), and a cord or string of flowers for the binding of the hands.

The Altar

The altar is set up with two pink candles (one on each side) and a union candle in the center. It also has two sticks of incense—one jasmine, one musk—to represent the bride and groom, respectively.

To the left of the altar is a brazier with burning charcoal. The chalice goes in front of the union candle, and the elemental tokens go on the right side, along with the bowl of rose petals.

The Ritual

(An invocation is absent here due to the fact that sacred space is "pre-set." Also note that this particular Wedding took place outdoors. Change the wording if you use this for an indoor ritual.)

The parents of those being wed come down the aisle and light their child's individual candle and incense, then take seats. The customary processional follows, with the couple walking in together followed by a swordbearer. The swordbearer symbolically protects the couple from any mundane or spiritual danger. The swordbearer places the blade on the ground behind the couple then steps to one side.

The priest or priestess begins: *"A great bard once said that the groves were the gods' first temples, so it is fitting that family and friends are gathered here today, in Nature's temple, to witness and support the union of _____ and _____. We thank all of you for coming to share in this, the first day of what will be a lifetime adventure of growing, learning, and loving."* The minister picks up the small bowl of rose petals and begins moving clockwise around the couple while speaking.

"May thy love be as sweet and light as these petals to the four winds. Let them carry thy wishes of joy and harmony to the farthest corners of creation, and encircle thee both with peace." The minister returns to the altar for prayer.

"Let us pray: Great God and Goddess whose breath formed all things, powers of creation, spirits of nature, guardians and guides, we ask for thy presence and blessing in the sacred space. Bend down thy ears and hearken unto the vows that _____ and _____ exchange. Bear witness to the truth of their intentions. Celebrate with us this declaration of their union, which already exists in their hearts, and help them ever to walk the path of beauty in confidence together. So mote it be.

"Pray, good gentles, take what comfort you may in this hall where the sky is our ceiling, and the grass carpets our floor." The guests take their seats.

The minister turns to the couple, saying: *"Thy marriage is the continuation of a great journey, the path of which leads to thine hearts. The old life is about to be transformed and a new one begun. So, I ask thee now, what words indicate your desire?"*

The couple respond together: *"To be joined as one with the blessings of the God and Goddess."*

The minister asks: *"And what words do you bring with thee to this sacred altar to represent thy intentions?"*

The bride and groom answer together: *"Perfect love and perfect trust."*

The minister responds, *"No better words could be chosen for the beginning of a life together. And what tokens have thee brought to the altar to symbolize thy hopes for this relationship and all that thee give to it?"*

The bride and groom open and read their scrolls explaining the token each has chosen, which up to now has remained a secret. They exchange the tokens and hand the scrolls to the minister, who puts them in the brazier of coals, saying: *"Sacred Powers, pray heed and accept these words, prayers, and promises as they travel swiftly through time and space. What fire consumes, none may undo."*

At this point a reading chosen by the couple, and performed by a friend or family member, may occur.

The minister begins speaking again after the reading: *"In the beginning of our world, the God and Goddess gave humankind five elements to nurture us physically, enrich us mentally, and teach us spiritual truths. The air, represented here by incense, fills us with vital breath, and gives flight to our hopes and dreams. It teaches the lesson of creativity and flexibility so you may grow together despite the winds of change."* The minister places a pinch of powdered incense into an open sachet.

"Water, represented by a seashell, reminds thee to flow with life's ever moving current gently, to rain our feelings lightly on one another so as to nourish and refresh." The minister places a seashell into the open sachet.

"Earth, represented by this stone, is thy foundation; a place upon which to begin building thine relationship one step at a time." The minister places a stone into the open sachet.

"Fire, symbolized by this match, purifies and energizes thy efforts, bringing passion and the brilliant light of truth." The minister places the match in the open sachet.

"Finally, Spirit, symbolized by this white string, rejoices the soul and binds all things together into the spark of magic through the law of love." The minister ties up the sachet and gives it to the bride.

————, *I give this sachet into your keeping, as from the days of old women tended the sacred hearth, the heart of a home. Place this close* to this warmth that thy home, that thy lives together may be bountifully blessed by all these lessons of the Old Ones."

At this point another reading begins, chosen by the couple.

After the second reading, the minister begins again: "In ancient days, cups adorned altars around the world to honor the Sacred Powers of all creation. This nectar is made from peaches, the fruit of longevity, wisdom, and joy that thy relationship may eternally be filled with discernment and happiness."

The minister holds the cup high toward the sky, saying: "Lord of Wine and Wonder, Lady of Canticles and Creation, bless this cup and the nectar therein, representing wisdom and everlasting love. Once taken to lips, let this unite these two into a oneness of hand, heart, spirit, and destiny." The bride and groom sip from the cup, then give the rest to the land so love may grow.

The minister now begins to declare the couple's vows line by line. These are generally written by the couple. After both the bride and groom have recited their vows, the minister challenges the bride: "I ask thee for once and always, _____, before the Ancient Ones, friends and family, and the sacred altar if it is still thy heartfelt wish to freely give love, passion, and gentility to this man. If so, say, 'By my honor let it be so.'"

The bride responds.

Then to the groom: "I ask thee _____, for once and always, before the Ancient Ones, friends and family, and the sacred altar if it is still thy heartfelt wish to freely give love, passion, and gentility to this woman. If so, say, 'By my honor let it be so.'"

The groom responds.

The minister picks up the rings from the altar. "May these rings be blessed as the symbol of affectionate unity, joining the lives of _____ and _____ in an unbroken circle. Wherever these two go, may they always return to one another in togetherness, finding the love for which all men and women yearn. May _____ and _____ grow in understanding and compassion, may their home be a sanctuary for love and friendship. May these rings, now placed upon their fingers, symbolize the touch of spirit, and the love in their hearts."

The minister gives instructions to the couple individually, beginning with the groom: "_____, place the ring of fulfillment and commitment on _____'s finger, saying, 'With this ring I pledge my love.'" This procedure is repeated for the bride.

The minister speaks to the bride and groom: "Before thee are three candles, two of which represent the two of thee. From every human being there is a light that reaches ever toward enlightenment. When two loving souls find one another, this light flows together in brilliance and beauty from their oneness. Light now the central candle; ignite it with the refreshing aroma of thy love." The bride and groom light the central candle using their individual candles as a fire source. The individual candles remain lit.

The minister continues: "This light symbolizes the presence of Spirit that has brought _____ and _____ together, and the unconditional love and trust they have pledged. The other two candles remain lit, as marriage is not the loss of individuality but a new horizon for each. From today forward the two of thee shall grow into the sacred We, where without the other there would be less than one."

The third reading chosen by the couple takes place now.

The minister gives the nuptial blessing: "May the blessings of life, the joys of love, the peace of truth, the wisdom of the soul, and the strength of the Spirit be thy constant companions now and always. So mote it be.

"I present to thee now the gift of bread, as our ancestors did, that thee might never want for physical or spiritual sustenance, and so that thy life together will be fruitful." The bride and groom each eat a piece. "Share this now with thy guests that they too might savor the sweetness of your joy, share in the Earth's providence and the blessings of the Divine." The couple begin handing out rolls, or perhaps pass them to some children present who can help with this task.

After everyone has eaten, the minister continues: "Good gentles, stand, and let us pray. God and Goddess, spirits of Sky and Stone, Water and Sun, we thank thee for thy presence and blessings this day. Like the stars above, let love be constant. Like the stone, let it be firm and unwavering. Like the water, let it flow between these two, and like the sun, let it ever be warm and welcoming. We ask as we go from this place that thee will keep watch and vigil over this couple and the sanctity of their union. So mote it be."

The minister takes a rope or floral strand to bind the outside hands of each person (e.g., the man's right and the woman's left) together while saying, "With the exchange of rings, the support of friends and family, under the gaze of the Ancestors and with the blessings of the God and Goddess, thee hast declared and accepted each other's offerings of eternal love. Your lives are now bound together in body, heart, mind, and soul. As you go now from this place, enter into a new life of beauty, joy and abundance together, marked by your passage across this sword which has protected you. Blessed be."

The minister turns the couple to face the gathering. They jump the sword. Traditionally, this marks their new life together and ensures figurative or literal fertility.

The minister speaks to the assembly: "Having pledged their troth before all Sacred Powers, it is now our duty as friends and family to support this couple on their path in life. Good gentles all, please welcome Mr. and Mrs. _____." The bride and groom walk down the aisle. The sword bearer takes up the blade and follows them out.

Postritual Foods

These depend a lot on the reception the couple have planned, but one traditional choice is candied almonds for sweet, abiding love.

18

Handfasting Ritual

Preparations

Decorate the circle with horseshoes at each of the four quarters, along with a red or pink candle to represent love, already ignited. Besides this, gather together a candle to represent the Ancients, flower petals, sea salt, rose oil, a bell, a broom, and a goblet of red wine.

The Altar

Put two circlets of flowers on the altar, one on each side. Have sea salt mingled with flower petals in a bowl to the right of the altar, and rose anointing oil to the left. The Ancients' candle goes in the center, and is burning at the outset. Sea salt and the wine can go anywhere visually pleasing. Have the broom leaning on one side.

Invocation

The sea salt and flowers are tossed to form the circle's perimeter while the officiant recites the invocation. This is best chosen or written by the couple.

The Ritual

The couple stand before the altar to be greeted by the presiding priest or priestess, and anointed with the oil of love. The officiant raises the circle of flowers above the woman's head, saying: *"Father of the Morning Sky, Sister of the Silver Star, attest to the Handfasting of these young hearts. May the binding of this union be felt as strongly as their bonds with the Mother. It is a bond of love equally shared."*

The officiant raises the second circlet above the man's head, saying, *"Father of the Early Sun, Sister of the Swelling Sea, attest to the Handfasting of these young hearts. May thy light and fertile water flow into their hearts to nourish the love that abides there."*

The officiant speaks to the couple: *"I tell thee now, that this is the law. That thou loves all things in Nature as the gifts of the Ancients. That thou harm none by word or deed. That thou go modestly through this life and not stray from the path. Content shall thou find in the small things of this life, and at last thou will meet again in the next; your destinies are linked."*

The officiant takes the cup of wine, saying, *"This cup of wine represents life's blood. By drinking of this you freely join your lives together."* The couple share the cup.

"Hear thee well. The spirits of all creation witness your choice, from the simplest stone to the cloak of stars above. With this blood bond made, none can separate thee other than the gods and thyselves."

Other Activities

The couple can exchange specific vows with each other at this point in the ritual. It is also nice to pass a talking stick around the circle so that all participants can share their hopes and wishes for the couple in an intimate way.

Closing the Circle

The officiant begins in the north, introducing the couple to the elements and ringing a bell, after which the couple blow out that quarter's candle.

NORTH

Guardians and Guides of the Rich Earth, witness this couple's promise and bless them with abundance.

EAST

Guardians and Guides of the Refreshing Winds, witness this couple's promise and bless them with sensitivity.

SOUTH

Guardians and Guides of the Empowering Fires, witness this couple's promise and bless them with passion.

WEST

Guardians and Guides of the Flowing Waters, witness this couples promise and bless them with pure love.

CENTER

Guardians and Guides of the Magic Realms, witness this couple's promise and bless them with unity of heart and soul. So mote it be.

The broomstick is placed on the floor for the couple to jump over, then the cakes and wine are blessed and shared among all the participants.

19

The Blessingway

Preparing for the birth of a child is exciting, but the parents-to-be can also discover that they have many conflicting feelings, some of which are concerns over being a "good" parent. In Wicca, Blessingways and Parenting Rituals are designed specifically to give the parents-to-be a forum in which they can discuss these feelings with other parents. The ritual also includes an opportunity to pamper the couple, a diversion for which they will soon have little time!

In terms of timing, hold the Blessingway and Parenting Rituals approximately three months before the birth of the child.

The following ritual was performed for Sharon, and is shared here with thanks to Colleen Koziara.

Preparations

Strew the circle with calming herbs such as lavender, and other scents that the mother-to-be prefers. Have a comfortable chair for the mother-to-be, some beverages and food, and any items that you need for the caring rituals described in "Other Activities," below. You also need a special robe for the mother-to-be, a crown of flowers, and any gifts to be presented to the parents.

The Altar

One white candle is sufficient to represent the Sacred. Also have individual candles for the mother and father, and one small one that represents the baby. Gifts for the parents and the crown of flowers can also rest here.

Invocation

If possible, this ritual should be performed during a full moon, a symbol of fruitfulness and maturity. This invocation starts in the east, the region of new beginnings. While walking, the person performing the invocation can strew herbs and/or flowers. The goddess invoked can be changed, but call on one who represents fertility and motherhood.

Note that this ritual begins with only women in the circle. The father-to-be waits outside the circle until escorted in. If you wish the father to be present, then special activities need to be added for his caring ritual, which should be handled by other fathers.

We call to you Demeter, Mother of All; on this the Full Moon, we honor your power. Demeter, the goddess who knows where in space we are at all times. You are a mantle to the universe; a sensor set on eternity. Your life is bound together with ours. You are our nourisher, the life that gave us life. We, women all, have gathered in your presence, to honor one who is nourishing and growing a new life; one soon to experience the birth of a soul...the soul of a child new to this world. This mother is about to become the nourisher, the oldest, most powerful way of being. She will nurture, care, and protect. The soul of the mother is unfathomable—capable of boundless love, yet often forgotten in modern times.

A mother is tender, taking a frightened infant to her breast. She comforts her child, chasing away fear and hurt with passion. Strong, she will realize the power within herself to meet each new challenge with a smile and soft words of encouragement. She will protect her child in any way necessary, and understand why the most dangerous creatures in the world are mothers protecting their young.

We maidens and mothers give honor to this woman of your spirit, who walks a path of transformation. Let your spirit be present here, that we may know ourselves as nurturers of the world's children, and caretakers of Earth's future. As we give of ourselves to this mother-to-be, help us each realize our power as co-creators. Blessed be the spirit of Demeter, among us and within us.

Meditation and Visualization

The mother-to-be is presented with a special garment at this point. She is bathed or anointed with fragrant oils, then guided through a visualization in which she can commune with the spirit of her unborn child. The person reading this should pause regularly, giving the mother-to-be time to go deeply into the meditation and integrate the words.

Close your eyes and breathe deeply, and evenly. Relax. Know that you are safe here among friends and in the company of the Sacred Powers. As you feel any fears and tensions slipping easily away from you, direct your attention within. Feel the life in your belly moving; dancing with its own waltz. Its heart beats full and strong. Know that your body sustains this miracle. It is part of you.

Look within. Follow the energy of your life force through your navel, through the umbilical cord, to the baby. Greet it with arms of spirit, and hold it close to yourself. This is your child, a life within a life. This is a spirit who has come to you to learn and grow. Welcome it within you; welcome it and wrap it with love.

The Ritual

The main body of the ritual begins with any of the caring rituals described in "Other Activities," then goes on to welcome the father-to-be in the sacred space.

The father-to-be is escorted into the circle. If for any reason no father is present, the woman's birth coach is a good substitute. This person picks up the crown of flowers, saying, *"You who sits upon the throne of the Lady, listen and look within. Know your power. Know that you embody the creative forces of Nature, the most powerful force in the universe."* The flowers are placed on the woman's head.

The person leading this ritual then stands before the altar, lighting the candle of the Sacred, saying, *"Hear ye the words of the Star Goddess, she whose feet are the host of heaven, and whose body encircles the universe.*

"I am the beauty and the green Earth; the white moon among the stars, and the desires within the hearts of all people. I call unto your soul. Arise and come to me! I am the song of Nature, who sings life into the universe. From me all things proceed, and to me all things return. Let your innermost self be enfolded in the rapture of the infinite; let my worship be in your heart.

"The acts of love and pleasure are my rituals. Let there be beauty, power, strength, compassion, honor, humility, mirth, and reverence within you. Know too that when you seek me, look within, for that is the greatest of all mysteries. I have been with you from the beginning, and I am the attainment of your heart's desire. Be welcome here, and be blessed."

The leader turns to the father now. "You who chose the path of fatherhood, know that you are here to comfort the mother and child, and to provide a strong but gentle hand; to be friend and protector. Speak now the words of the God!"

The father turns to the altar saying, "I am the stag of the wind and waters; a shining tear of the sun, a hawk on the cliffs, a battle-waged spear, a salmon in a pool. I call unto your soul. Arise and come unto me. I am the Father of the Heavens. Forgotten are the way of sleep and night, open this door…the door without a key that leads back to me. I am the Father of the Sky, the Lord of the Hunt, the Green Man of the Woods…with you from the beginning, and within you now. Be welcome and blessed."

Those who have brought gifts present them now, with any appropriate explanations.

Other Activities

The mother-to-be may receive a full-body massage, manicure, pedicure, facial, or body painting as part of the caring ritual. This is a time for her to be pampered lavishly, and relax in the company of friends. As the caring continues, she can openly discuss her fears and concerns, and share her joy with other women.

To divine the sex of the baby, just for fun, use a pendulum. Hold this steady over the woman's stomach. If the pendulum swings in circles, it represents a boy; ellipses, a girl.

One especially appropriate activity is hairstyling. In earlier times, a change in hairstyle often marked important spiritual transformations. For example, the cutting of hair among monks and nuns shows their commitment to a new, unmaterialistic life. Similarly, the woman's hair can be changed somehow to mark her new role as a mother.

Closing the Circle

Farewell Demeter; Farewell Father Sky and Mother Earth. We thank you for blessing these parents-to-be, and for joining us in this circle. Be with these two now. Grant them wisdom, insight, strength, and gentility so that the soul that is their child will know all the wonders of magic and love. When the baby is born, let it bring joy into their lives, and new growth. Watch over them now, and us as we leave this place. The circle, while open, is not broken within our hearts. So be it.

Postritual Foods

Consider anything that has a maternal or lunar association, such as milk or a cauliflower puff pastry. Don't forget any foods the mother has been craving!

20

Parenting Ritual

This ritual bears many similarities to the Blessingway except that it is more focused on both parents. Note that the ritual should be modified for single mothers, perhaps by using a birthing partner or close friend as the other participant in the activities.

Preparations

This ritual can be combined with a "shower" for the parents, so those attending should bring appropriate gifts. Decorations should be bright and lively, full of the spirit of celebration. Have colored candles and symbols at the quarter points ready for the invocation, along with a length of yellow ribbon or a feather (east), bread (north), a cup with sweetened milk (west), and incense (south).

The Altar

Cover the altar with a yellow cloth, the color of creativity, or possibly a green cloth for growth. Have one central candle (unlit) to represent the Spirit. Gifts for the couple can be placed here to absorb the positive energy generated by the ritual.

Invocation

The leader of this ritual speaks to those gathered before the invocation, saying, *"We are here to honor these people, about to become parents. We rejoice for them, and for all of us, in welcoming a new spirit to Earth. In some ways we are all parents—caretakers of Earth and all that lives thereon. We also guide our inner child on the path of beauty."*

The leader moves to the eastern quarter and lights the candle there. *"Spirit of the Wind, the Great Bird of Creation, open your wings and protect us. Grant us your perception and vision. Be with us in this circle."*

Moving to the SOUTH, the leader lights the candle there, saying, *"Spirit of the Fire, Great Lion of the Sun, ignite your fires within us. Bring passion, strength, and guidance to this gathering. Be with us now."*

Moving to the WEST, the leader lights the candle there, saying, *"Spirit of the Water, Great Fish of the World's Oceans, let love flow within and around us. Bring joy, harmony, and wisdom on your waves. Be with us now."*

Moving to the NORTH, the leader lights the candle there, saying, *"Spirit of the Earth, Great Mother of All Things, let nurturing flow from your breast. Bring your power and fruitfulness to all here gathered. Be with us now."*

Finally, the leader lights the central candle, saying, *"Spirit of Beginnings, Great Powers of Creation, we entreat your presence. Be with us now."*

Meditation and Visualization

The meditation for the Parenting Ritual can be similar to the one for the Blessingway, except that both parents should be encouraged to connect with the child's spirit. In this case, have the couple sit facing each other, both holding their hands over the woman's stomach. Make other appropriate changes to the guided meditation, one example of which follows:

*Close your eyes and breathe deeply, and evenly. Relax. Know that
you are safe here among friends and in the company of the Sacred
Powers. As you feel any fears and tensions slipping easily away
from you, direct your attention to this woman's womb. Feel the life
there moving; dancing with it's own waltz. Its heart beats full and
strong. This child is part of both of you, conceived of one united
heart.*

*Look within. Follow the energy of life through your hands, to the
navel, through the umbilical cord, to the baby. Extend your aura to
wrap the child with arms of spirit, and hold it close to yourself. This
is your baby, whom you give life. This is a spirit who has come to
you to learn and grow. Welcome it; welcome it and wrap it with
love.*

The Ritual

The leader now turns his or her attention to the couple, saying,
*"You two are about to embark on a great adventure. Are you ready for
all the responsibilities to come?"*

The couple respond: *"We are ready to do our best."*

Leader: *"This child comes to this world helpless, but for your love
and support. Are you ready to freely give these things?"*

Couple: *"We are, with all our hearts."*

The leader takes the couple to the four quarters, beginning in
the east. *"Powers of the Air, witness these two who are about to become
parents. Give them the gift of insight, and the courage to let their child
fly free when the time comes."* The leader gives the couple a feather.
"Let truth guide you."

The couple move to the south with the leader. *"Powers of Fire,
witness these two about to become parents. Your gift of passion
generated life, now keep those loving fires burning* [hands the couple
a stick of incense] *and give them the energy needed to endure the
months ahead."*

The couple move to the west with the leader. *"Powers of Water,
witness these two about to become parents. Grant them steady hearts,*

and level heads as they bring up this child. [The leader gives them the cup from which they both drink.] *Let the sweet milk of the Mother grant their spirits sustenance."*

Finally, all move to the north. *"Powers of Earth, witness these two about to become parents. Grant them sure foundations to weather all storms that may come.* [The leader gives them bread, which they both eat.] *Let the bread of life grant them both perseverance for the days ahead."*

The leader turns to the father, saying, *"Father, what is your wish?"*

The father responds, *"To care for my child, and this woman who has given it life."*

Leader: *"Mother, what is your wish?"*

Mother: *"To give this child life and care for it with this man, whose seed helped create it."*

The leader raises his or her hands in blessing. *"Powers of Creation, God and Goddess, bless these two and hear their prayer. Unite them in joy and love in the bringing up of this child yet to be born. So be it."*

Other Activities

Allow those gathered to share their personal experiences with children, and any helpful hints they might have, at this juncture. Also have them present their gifts to the couple, with any explanation of the symbolism (if necessary).

Closing the Circle

NORTH
Mother Earth, we thank you for your blessings and abundance, and bid you farewell.

WEST
Sister Water, we thank you for your blessings and insight, and bid you farewell.

SOUTH

Father Fire, we thank you for your blessings and power, and bid you farewell.

EAST

Brother Wind, we thank you for your blessings and breath of life, and bid you farewell.

CENTER

Great Spirit, we thank you for your blessings and the gift of this child, and bid you farewell.

21

Birth or Adoption (Wiccaning)

When a new child comes into a home, it begins a whole new cycle in everyone's lives. Suddenly there is a small spirit who needs undivided love and attention. And while the effort can seem arduous at times, it has amazing, unquantifiable rewards. Just look at the expression on every parents' face the first time their baby smiles.

The purpose of a Wiccaning Ritual is to welcome the child as a part of the family, and thank the Powers. It also introduces the baby to all the elemental powers for blessing and protection. This particular Wiccaning comes from Colleen Koziara, as performed for Hannah in 1991. Consider holding this ritual at the first signs of a crescent moon, so the child may grow and thrive like the increasing moon. The themes of this ritual are hope, joy, and thankfulness.

Preparations

Decorate the four quarters with baby items that somehow depict the energies of that space. For example, diapers can represent

Earth, a rattle, Air, a blanket, Fire, and a bottle, Water. Have white candles at the quarter points to represent new life.

The Altar

As with the quarter points, the altar is covered in white, for beginnings. If you plan to bless the baby with the elements (see "Other Activities"), a cup of water, a smudge stick, a cup of soil, and a feather should be decoratively laid out here, too.

Invocation

This invocation starts in the east, where the sun rises with joy and hope on this special occasion.

EAST
Lord of the Winds, come dance and play,
for we welcome here a child this day.

SOUTH
Lord of the Fire, come shine and spark
that this child's path will ne'er be dark.

WEST
Lady of the Water, come by wave and dew
that this child's tears will only be few.

NORTH
Lady of the Earth, come by soil and sand,
give this child your helping hand.

CENTER
Spirit of Creation, come in truth and love
that this child may be blessed by all Powers above.

Meditation and Visualization

Although not necessary to the ritual, one idea might be to write a guided meditation that extends loving, warm energy into the room for the child. One example follows. (Make sure to put pauses in periodically so that the participants have time to fix the imagery and direct the magic):

Close your eyes and breathe deeply. From overhead, see the clean, white light of the Spirit pouring into this place, and into your heart. Allow this to warm you and fill you to overflowing. When you sense the energy reaching a pinnacle within, direct it outward. Visualize this energy forming a pink sphere of love and joy around this sacred space. Think of the child here with us, and your feelings toward him/her. Give all your love and support to that sphere so he/she is surrounded by the blessing of perfect love.

The Ritual

The leader begins, "*We greet one who is new to this Earth. We present this small and sacred one to the Old Gods, and welcome him/her among us. Who is it that shall come before the Gods?*"

The parents respond: "*We do.*"

The leader continues: *And how shall this child be known to his/her brothers and sisters of the Old Ways?*" The mother of the child responds with the child's magical name. "*And who speaks for this small one?*"

The mother says, "*Before our friends, before those of the mysteries, before all seen and unseen, before the powers of Earth, Wind, Fire, and Sea, and before the Ancient Ones. Before the Lord and Lady themselves do we bring forth* _____ [real name of child] *who shall be known as* _____ [magical name] *whose spirit found us, and whom we brought forth in love.*

The leader lays hands on the baby, saying, "*May the blessings of the wise and joyous Father of the Gods, far-seeing and far-knowing, be upon thee, small friend!*" *May the blessings of the Triple Goddess, of Maiden, Mother, and Crone, and all of their power be upon thee, small friend!*" (It should be noted that in some traditions the blessing of the God is given by a priest, while that for the Goddess is performed by a priestess.)

The leader then turns to the parents with the following exhortations. (If two people perform this rite, the priest goes first, followed by the priestess, and so forth.)

I bid you both hearken to my words. For the bringing of a new life into the world and the linking of one so young to the most Ancient Ways is a serious matter.

I bid you both to give your child the finest and deepest training, yet make not his/her life one of tedious labor. One so young must live well the joys of life.

I bid you both to give your child a home of warmth and gentleness. If you have differences, moderate them so that his/her world knows no disruption.

I bid you both to respect your child as an individual, for he/she is unique. Remember always that a small frame and a child's ways often cover a fine mind that in later years many shall honor.

I bid you both to give always a fair hearing to your child. Have patience, as he/she learns and asks, and remember that you yourselves once walked his/her path.

I bid you both to give ever new horizons, new challenges, new worlds, so that your child may go so far as his/her own mind and spirit shall lead. Do you hearken to these words?

The parents respond, *"We do."*

The leader continues, *"If you are ready to assume these duties as parents of a child of the Old Ones, then take these vows and repeat after me: We _____, as parents and followers of the Old Ways, do take this sacred vow, before the Lord and Lady, to whom we give honor."* The parents repeat the vow together.

Leader: *"You who would be godparent(s) to this child, come forth."* The godparent(s) joins the parents before the altar. *"Are you ready to assume the duties as godparent to this child to aid the parents in his/her upbringing; to support the child that he/she may grow in knowledge and love? Are you ready to assume these responsibilities?"*

The godparent(s) replies, *"I am. I assume these duties in the name of the Lord, the Lady, and the Ancient Ones."*

The leader begins to walk the couple, child, and godparent(s) around the circle clockwise, saying, *"As we walk the circle of power and light, we ask that the elements bless this life, that it may be rich and joyful. We ask the powers to witness this rite by which* _____ *has been dedicated to the Sacred and to the Craft."* The leader now returns to the center of the circle and closes the ritual.

Other Activities

As the parents walk around the circle with the child, they introduce him or her to the elemental powers. As the leader speaks each part of this blessing, they touch the child's hand to the element; in the case of the smudge stick, the smoke is simply moved into the baby's aura. (Caution: be sure to keep it minimal so the baby doesn't start coughing.)

EAST
Of Air and inspiration, the morning winds,
come ye Powers of the east.
Bless and protect this child
as our rite begins.

SOUTH
Of Fire and power, the noon sun,
come ye Powers of the south.
Bless and protect this child;
the magic is begun.

WEST
Of Water and insight, the evening tides,
come ye Powers of the west.
Bless and protect this child
and in his/her heart abide.

NORTH
Of Earth and growth, the midnight loam,
come ye Powers of the north.
Bless and protect this child
that he/she knows you as his/her home.

Another nice activity suggested for this ritual is for everyone present to bring a small token for the baby. These will all become part of the child's medicine bag, which is returned either upon initiation or at the Rite of Adulthood.

Closing the Circle

Instead of a closing invocation, this ritual has a prayer. *"O gracious Lord and Lady, whose hands turn the vast sky, and in whom all things begin and end throughout eternity, thank you for this life that has been dedicated to you. Blessed be."*

The members of the group repeat, *"Blessed be."*

Postritual Foods

I suggest light, easy-to-prepare and -eat finger foods. Wiccaning and other types of Dedication Rituals are usually followed by lots of socializing, so edibles need to be portable.

22

Birthdays

One day out of the year you are the most important person in the world—on your birthday. Birthdays mark our time on this planet, our learning and growing, and our failures and successes along the way. They are an excellent occasion to perform the Ritual of Self-Dedication again (see part 1); to ponder where life is taking us, and how our spirituality will be honored on that road. The themes of this ritual are thankfulness, thoughtfulness, and hope.

Preparations

The celebrant should invite friends and family to share this day. Have elementally colored balloons marking the perimeter of the circle for a festive flair. Besides this you will need a specially prepared anointing oil—the scent and significance chosen by the celebrant—a birthday cake, a long-handled match, candles (to represent the Spirit), and a cup with wine or juice.

The Altar

Adorn the altar with the celebrant's favorite colors. Place a birthday cake in the center of the sacred candles, which are lit. Put a cup of wine or juice on one side, the anointing oil on the other; scatter any gifts decoratively around the base.

Invocation

Birthdays mark a full turning of the Wheel, so begin your invocation in the north, where the clock begins anew.

NORTH

Hail, powers of the Earth. Join this circle and celebrate the birthday of _____. *We give thanks to for the rich soil that you have provided for him/her to grow in. Watch over us now as we join together to rejoice in this life, its continuance, and the seeds of magic he/she bears.*

EAST

Hail, Powers of the Air. Join this circle and celebrate the birthday of _____. *We give thanks for the winds of change that have motivated him/her toward wonders and wisdom. Watch over us now as we join together to rejoice in this life, and the breath of magic he/she bears.*

SOUTH

Hail, Powers of the Fire. Join this circle and celebrate the birthday of _____. *We give thanks for the sparks of energy that have sustained him/her throughout this last year. Watch over us now as we join together to rejoice in this life, and the ember of magic he/she bears.*

WEST

Hail, Powers of the Water. Join this circle and celebrate the birthday of _____. *We give thanks for the waves of joy and creativity that have filled his/her life this year. Watch over us now as we join together to rejoice in this life, and the wellspring of magic he/she bears.*

CENTER

The center invocation should be written and performed by the celebrant, in thanks for his or her blessings, and to voice any personal needs and goals for the coming year.

Meditation and Visualization

This meditation centers on the celebrant, but also acts as a useful time of reflection for all those gathered:

Relax. Shed the cloak of the world. Let your tensions pour away. Let the world fade away...until nothing exists but you and the Sacred. Now go back in time to twelve months ago. See yourself as you were on that day. Think of the year that has passed...remember the happiness, the sorrow, the changes and growth experienced. Take a moment and remember it all, and accept it into yourself. These experiences are all part of you, of who you've become today, and who you will be tomorrow.

Observe the important moments in this year like a movie on the screen of your soul. Laugh with yourself; cry with yourself; and know both to be healthy and necessary. [Pause for an extended time to allow these things to flow through the participant's minds.]

Now we are here, today. You are a new person, born yet again with the dawn tomorrow. Welcome the person you've become. Hug yourself; hold close your auric energy that sustains your spirit. Love yourself perfectly, and vow to look toward tomorrow with hope in your heart.

The Ritual

The leader turns to the celebrant, saying, "Welcome, _____. *This is your special day, and we honor you. Today the Old Ones returned your spirit to Earth to learn and grow closer to enlightenment. This is indeed reason to rejoice!*"

The leader picks up the anointing oil and dabs it on the celebrant in the indicated spots while saying, "*May the year ahead be blessed with good thoughts and keen perceptions* [head]. *May the year ahead have little sadness, but instead fill you with joy* [heart]. *May the year ahead lead you farther along the path of beauty than ever before* [feet]."

The leader gives a long match to the celebrant, ignited from the candle(s) representing the Sacred. *"Light the candles of your cake with the wishes of your heart, then blow them out to send those prayers to the heavens."* The celebrant lights the cake and makes wishes, then everyone sings. This raises and directs positive energy directed toward the celebrant.

Other Activities

All those who have brought gifts present these to the celebrant, with their wishes and hopes. They can also take a moment to share a special, personal memory from the celebrant's past year.

Closing the Circle

WEST
'Round, and 'round, and 'round it goes,
follow where the water flows
from out this place, throughout the Earth
to honor _____'s day of birth.

SOUTH
'Round, and 'round, and 'round it turns,
follow where the fire burns
from out this place, throughout the dark,
carry safe our magic's spark.

EAST
'Round, and 'round, and 'round it spins,
follow where the winds begin
from out this place, throughout the air,
and on the breeze, the magic bear.

NORTH
'Round, and 'round, and 'round it twirls,
follow where the seeds unfurl
from out this place, throughout the land,
while in this sacred space, we stand.

CENTER
'Round, and 'round, and 'round it goes,
where it stops, Spirit knows.
Bless this life as his/her Wheel turns
and within him/her let the magic burn.
So mote it be.

Postritual Foods

Birthday cake, of course, and any items requested by the celebrant.

23

Separation

Great is the art of beginning, but greater the art
of ending.
—Henry Wadsworth Longfellow

With all the chaos and pressures of our world, more relationships are suffering, some to the point of separation and divorce. From a Wiccan perspective, this need not be a time of anger and retribution. As the old saying goes, "It takes two." Instead, in Wiccan traditions people often try to find positive ways to release each other from a failed relationship in the safety of a magical circle, either alone or joined by supportive friends. Consider holding this ritual during the time of a waning moon, to represent the dissolution of ties. The themes of this ritual are healing and releasing the past.

Preparations

Gather a long piece of ribbon (about five yards), a pair of scissors, three candles, a picture of the couple, and single photographs of each of them. The single photographs are placed in the eastern and western quarters, along with any other ritual tools desired. Before the ritual begins the couple is bound together with the ribbon, and they stand or sit before the altar.

The Altar

Cover the altar in a two-toned cloth, one half dark and the other light, to represent both endings and beginnings. Place the three candles evenly in the center of the altar, with the middle one lit before the picture of the couple. The scissors need to be near the front, easily accessible to the couple.

Invocation

This invocation begins in the west, the traditional region of death, to represent the ending of this cycle in the participant's lives.

WEST
Powers of the West, we call you to bear witness to this parting. Let your gentle waters begin to heal these two hearts.

SOUTH
Powers of the South, we call you to bear witness to this parting. Let your fires burn away any residual anger, and replace it with gentle warmth and understanding.

EAST
Powers of the East, we call you to bear witness to this parting. Let your winds of change blow freely here, bringing cool headedness and smooth transformations.

NORTH
Powers of the North, we call you to bear witness to this parting. Let your nurturing soils give these two souls a new plot of land in which to put down roots.

CENTER
Powers of Magic; Spirit of Beginnings and Endings, we call you to witness this parting. Bless these two as they close one door of their life, and open another.

Meditation and Visualization

This meditation is specifically designed for the couple.

Close your eyes and relax. Release your fears, your sadness, your worries... let them go. You don't need them anymore, for the Wheel is turning. When you feel relaxed, visualize the two of you as you stand right now. See how your auras intertwine; how they have mingled together. Slowly... gently... pull back the strands of energy that hold the two of you together... Bring back your essence into your heart chakra... until both of you stand as individuals, without any binds tying you together.

The Ritual

The leader begins with a charge to the couple: *"You have come into the circle of perfect love and trust, with intentions of peace. Is it still your wish to dissolve this relationship?"*

The couple respond, *"It is."*

The leader continues, *"Then cut loose the ribbons that bind you. As you cut, release your anger, release your bad memories, and hold dear those things that made you friends; it is as friends that you part."*

The couple together take the scissors and cut the ribbon, handing it to the leader of the ritual, who says, *"It is done."* He or she then hands each person a long match with which to light the single candles on each side of the altar. When these are ignited, the leader continues: *"You came into this coupling as individuals; the sacred We is dissolved by your choosing, but two individuals remain."* The leader blows out the central candle and takes down the couple's picture so it cannot be seen. *"Your lives will never be the same, having been touched by the other, yet today you return to apartness. Turn and walk away from this altar, carrying peace as your guide."*

The two people turn their backs to each other, walk to their singular pictures, and pick them up.

Other Activities

Purely personal. Ask the couple what would be most significant for them. For example, if the couple is getting a divorce, a glass goblet from their wedding might be broken during the ritual to represent the dissolution, or flowers from the bridal bouquet be burned.

Closing the Circle

This circle closes with a prayer. As the leader prays, the couple can remove the elemental tokens or blow out any candles, as desired.

Earth and Air; Fire and Sea; Powers of Eternity. Thank you for being with us in this place. Go now with _____ and _____ as they live apart. The path of the solitary is often long and hard, but it is also one filled with tremendous potential for personal growth. Let not their paths be filled with sadness or regrets. Let them not be bitter. Instead, let healing have its way, for today is a new day, and a new beginning for both of them. At it is witnessed in the sacred space, so let it be done! Farewell.

24

Forgiveness

Throughout the Wheel of Life there come moments that we all regret—times when words are harsh, or actions, hasty. Wiccans believe that performing a ritual to make amends gives everyone a chance to speak freely in a "roundtable" forum, and then heal those wounds using magic as a salve. Consider holding Forgiveness Rituals during the time of a waning-to-dark moon to represent decreasing hostilities, and a time to rest and heal wounds. The themes of this ritual are airing out problems; cleaning away the old; and release.

Preparations

Have each person bring several white daisies. Use white candles at the quarter points to symbolize peaceful intentions, and burn rose incense to inspire love instead of anger. You will also need a brazier or cauldron with burning coals that are already ignited at the start of the rite, and an empty basket or bowl.

The Altar

Keep the altar simple. Cover it with a pure white cloth (linen is a good choice), and have all participants place one of their daisies on the surface around the brazier or cauldron. This flower acts as a promise on that individual's part to leave anger outside the circle, and to work constructively on a resolution. The basket remains on the floor near the altar.

Invocation

If possible, everyone should chant the invocation while one person, who acts as a mediator, lights the quarter points. This invocation begins in the east, marking everyone's desire for a fresh start. Repeat the first line three times, then say the fourth in a whisper.

EAST
Come, Winds of Change! Come breathe on us!
Let peace be your guide.

SOUTH
Come, Fires of Awareness! Come spark in us!
Let peace here abide.

WEST
Come, Waters of Healing! Come flow through us!
Let peace grow inside.

NORTH
Come, Loam of Endings! Come draw out the pain
and in its place, bring joy again!

Meditation and Visualization

The mediator has all participants hold hands and close their eyes, then says:

Breathe deeply, in through your nose and out through your
mouth...one...two...one...two. As you breathe, draw in peace,
and release tension. Ground any fear or anger beneath your feet.
Give it to the Mother. She will turn it into soil in which resolution
grows. Release...release...release.
   Now, visualize this circle. See it surrounded by sparkling white

light. Envision your intentions of peace as one strand that reaches out to the center point of the circle. As you see this energy strand reach out from your heart, you also notice the strands from those here gathered. They unite in the middle of the circle, and twine together like clasped hands. Slowly, nearly imperceptibly, this knot of determination transforms. It grows wings. Your energies combined create a dove, who carries your strand of energy from this place to the Divine with our prayers. Release her to her duties.

The Ritual

The mediator takes up the basket and moves to the person standing due east of the circle, saying, *"What do you release?"* The participant then picks a petal off the flower he or she holds, naming the situation or feeling whose release is desired. He or she continues picking petals until all the issues are named.

The mediator moves counterclockwise (the direction of banishing) to the next person and repeats this procedure. This is continued until everyone has a turn. The mediator then goes to the brazier and says, *"Ancient Ones, see the intentions of those here gathered, and accept the negativity they have here released. These flames consume all pain and sorrow; they consume regrets. What is burned away is dead and buried forever."*

Beginning in the east again, the mediator returns to the first person, saying, *"What do you claim?"* That individual picks one flower petal for each positive thing he or she wishes to claim— "forgiveness," "peace," "healing," and so forth. This procedure is repeated for each participant clockwise around the circle for growing, affirmative energy.

The mediator then takes these petals and likewise burns them, saying, *"In ancient times people believed that sweet scents pleased the gods. May the Powers find the aroma of good intentions likewise pleasing. Accept these prayers and wishes, and use them as a salve to heal the wounds of all here present."*

The mediator turns to all those gathered and asks, *"Do you freely accept the forgiveness offered in this sacred space?"*

All participants answer in unison, *"We do."*
The mediator continues, *"Then let peace be with you."*

Other Activities

Before the actual ritual portion of the circle, the participants might conduct an open discussion of what happened, and why. The mediator watches over this discussion to make sure everyone gets a fair opportunity to speak, and that tempers don't get out of hand.

Closing the Circle

Begin in the western quarter to mark the end to dissension. Either the mediator or the group may perform the banishing.

WEST
Farewell, Spirits of Water! Farewell, Healing Waves! While you are apart from us, your drops of tranquillity remain.

SOUTH
Farewell, Spirits of Fire! Farewell, Cleansing Flames! While you are apart from us, your sparks of pure intention remain.

EAST
Farewell, Spirits of Air! Farewell, Refreshing Winds! While you are apart from us, your breeze of good motivations remains.

NORTH
Farewell, Spirits of Earth! Farewell, Soils of Birth! While you are apart from us, your loam of mature reasoning remains.

CENTER
Farewell, Great Ones! Farewell, Ancient Powers! While you are apart from us, your perfect love and trust remain. So mote it be.

Postritual Foods

How about a potluck feast to foster the spirit of cooperation?

25

Career Changes

One thing that Wiccan ritual attempts to accomplish is giving people an opportunity to integrate important changes in their lives. In our society, a person's career is very significant to his or her overall financial stability and sense of self-confidence. As career changes come, they offer challenges that are often accompanied by uncertainties. This ritual is meant to help ease those concerns. Consider holding it during a waxing moon, to represent your personal growth. The theme of this ritual is welcoming and integrating transformation.

Preparations

Into the sacred space bring clothing that somehow represents your new job. Use implements for the job to mark the four quarter points. For example, a secretary might use a paper clip to represent the Spirit (that which holds the magic together), a pencil for Earth (since it's made of wood), a coffee cup for Water, a telephone for Air (which rules communication), and a desk lamp for Fire.

Besides this you will need a container of water, a brazier or

cauldron with burning charcoal, a mirror (full length is best), and
a piece of paper upon which you've written out all your apprehen-
sions about the new position.

The Altar

Cover the altar in a pale yellow cloth to represent creative energy.
Place the cauldron and water container evenly apart on its surface,
the clothing at one side of the altar, and the paper on the other.

Invocation

This invocation begins in the east, the point of the rising sun, to
mark your new beginning.

EAST
Dance with the Wind, dance with the Air,
remove from me all worries and care!
Dance with the Air, dance with the Wind,
so my magic can begin!

SOUTH
Jump with the Flame, jump with the Fire,
my fears burn away in the magical pyre!
Jump with the Fire, jump with the Flame,
soon my life will ne'er be the same!

WEST
Flow with the Rain, flow with the Dew,
I welcome today, my life anew!
Flow with the Dew, flow with the Rain,
fears wash away, confidence gained!

NORTH
Grow with the Earth, grow with the Soil,
grant me wisdom all while I toil!
Grow with the Soil, grow with the Earth,
mark well this day, a day of rebirth!

CENTER

The invocation to the Spirit should take the form of a prayer that expresses your hopes for this job, and asks for divine blessings in your efforts.

Meditation and Visualization

Slowly put on the clothing you brought into the ritual space and stand before a mirror. As you put on each piece, claim one characteristic that you wish to take with you into this position—"confidence," "leadership ability," "organization," and so forth. When you have put on all the clothing, close your eyes and visualize yourself working successfully in your new capacity. Walk through an entire day of responsibilities, all of which are undertaken effectively. Then open your eyes and see the new person you're becoming!

The Ritual

Hold the piece of paper in your hands. Allow all of your anxieties to pour out onto that paper. Release them. Continue letting any fears drain away until you feel empty, with nothing but assurance left inside. Crumple the paper as you might a piece of garbage and release it to the fire, saying thrice:

> Burn, burn, burn;
> the Wheel turns, turns, turns;
> fears no more in me,
> confidence be free!

Other Activities

If there are any specific studies that could help you in the new job, take time to review these in the sacred space. Read, take notes, begin organizing your ideas on how to make yourself the most effective employee or boss possible.

Closing the Circle

NORTH
Farewell to Earth, from which all things grow.
As I leave from this place, nurture stability;
as above, so below.

WEST
Farewell to Water, from which all things flow.
As I leave from this place, inspire my soul.

SOUTH
Farewell to Fire, from which all things gain power.
As I leave from this place, this magical hour.

EAST
Farewell to Air, from which all things start.
As I leave from this place, refresh my heart.

CENTER
Farewell to Spirit, in which all things unite.
Be with me now, let my magic take flight!

Postritual Food

This depends on the job to which you're going. An office worker might choose doughnuts (a favorite Friday treat), for example. Or if there's a lunch restaurant near your new place of employment, eat out. You deserve a treat.

26

New Homes

Whether you're moving to an apartment or a house, this structure is an important sacred space. Of all areas in the world, home is the one where you can relax and truly be yourself. Consequently, regular maintenance of a home's spiritual vibrations is very important. House cleansing and blessings help keep these vibrations positive and life affirming. Consider holding this type of ritual during the time of a waxing or full moon for uplifting energy. The themes of this ritual are blessing and protection.

Preparations

Clean the entire apartment or home. Spiritually, this helps remove any lingering energies from previous occupants. Purchase a smudge stick or some cedar and sage incense. Gather a feather, a bowl of rose water, a small bell, and four elementally significant stones (for example, green agate for Earth, carnelian for Fire, a seashell for Water, and any white or yellow stone for Air). Use household decorations or knickknacks for the four quarters.

The Altar

Cover the altar with your favorite cloth. Place the feather and bowl of rose water at one side, the stones on the other, and the incense and bell in the middle. If desired, a picture of everyone in your family can also go on the altar to let the building know who will be abiding here, and who blesses it.

Invocation

Pick up the bowl of rose water and the feather, and use the feather to sprinkle the water around the entire home, moving clockwise, to douse it with love as you recite the invocation:

EAST
I stand at the threshold of time and space
and welcome ye Guardians of the Air.
Protect this house with loving care.

SOUTH
I stand here, before the noonday sun,
and welcome ye Guardians of the Hearth.
Purify this home, fill it ever with warmth.

WEST
I stand here, at the ocean's shore,
and welcome ye Guardians of the Sea.
Let love and health abide here with me.

NORTH
I stand here, rooted in rich earth,
and welcome ye Guardians of the Land.
Ward this place, take well your stand.

CENTER
I stand here, amid whirling magic,
and welcome the Lord and Lady into this place.
Bless it now, create a sacred space.
So mote it be.

Meditation and Visualization

Throughout your ritual, keep a strong image of sparkling white light filling every nook and cranny of your home. Don't forget windows, door cracks, heating ducts, and chimneys. Let this pure, protective energy saturate the walls, ceiling, and floor.

The Ritual

Next, light the smudge stick of incense. Again moving clockwise, go into each room of the house. In each major area, use the incense to draw three invoking pentagrams in the air (this begins at the upper left side of the star, and ends on the upper right). As you draw this image, imagine the white light of your visualization being part of it, and say:

> *Spirit of Magic, and Love, and Peace,*
> *protect this space, ne'er cease;*
> *within these walls no evil may dwell*
> *by the ringing of this bell.* [Ring the bell.]

Next, put the incense on the altar and pick up the leftover rose water from the invocation. Take this to the threshold of your home and pour it over the cornerstone or foundation, saying:

> *Guardians and Sacred Powers,*
> *watch over all comings and goings in this home;*
> *let peace, joy, health, and love freely enter here.*

Finally, return to the altar and place your hands over the four stones you gathered, saying, *"Great Spirit, bless these stones as symbolic of the elemental powers in all creation. Empower them to safeguard my home, and my sacred space. Fill them now to act as a shield of faith against all storms I may weather. By your power, through my will, so be it."*

Place the stones around your home in the direction whose element they represent. By so doing you have just created a semipermanent sacred space that will be activated and empowered during ritual invocations.

Other Activities

Consider turning out all the pilot lights in the house and relighting them. In ancient times, the hearth was the heart of a home. Your reignition of the pilots equates to bringing new life and love into that space.

Closing the Circle

NORTH
Earth of My Foundations, that holds firm my home, I thank you for participating in this rite and guarding the circle. Allow your magical roots to linger, watching over all those who seek refuge here.

WEST
Waters of Cleansing, that wash ever through this place, I thank you for participating in this rite and guarding the circle. Allow your healing waves to roll, making whole all those who seek refuge here.

SOUTH
Fires of My Creation, that burn ever in the hearth, I thank you for participating in this rite and guarding the circle. Allow your magical embers to linger, warming all those who seek refuge here.

EAST
Air of Insight, that breathes ever through my windows, I thank you for participating in this rite and guarding the circle. Allow your refreshing winds to invigorate all those who seek refuge here.

CENTER
Spirit of Truth and Perfect Love, be always a welcome guest in my home. Keep it filled with good thoughts, kind words, and constructive action. So be it.

Postritual Foods

Make your favorite dish (or dishes, if you have a family) and enjoy them buffet-style. Try to include an unsliced loaf of bread from which everyone can break a piece, or a single cup of nectar. Either of these symbolizes the unity in your home.

27

Eldership

Over the last century we have somehow lost sight of the fact that old does not necessarily mean outmoded or without purpose. The elders of our communities are a valuable resource. In Wicca, we honor our elders' accumulated wisdom and knowledge with a special ritual. While you can perform an Eldership Ritual alone to welcome aging, and the insights it brings, I feel this is better enacted in a group setting.

A group Eldership Ritual accomplishes several things. It lets the aging person know that his or her contribution is still necessary and valuable. It also singles out the elder to all those gathered as a source of rich insights and inspiration. This ritual might be done during a full moon to represent maturity. The themes of this ritual are wisdom and insight.

Preparations

Have all participants in this ritual bring one token with them. This token should represent something important that they learned from the celebrant. The person being recognized as an elder might wish to take a ritual bath in symbolic herbs, such as sage for wisdom and sandalwood for spiritual insight. Gather two candles to represent the God and Goddess, and one large central candle to symbolize the celebrant. If this ritual is performed in autumn, colorful leaves look lovely strewn around to mark the circle.

The Altar

Cover the altar in a shawl or other token that represents the Grandfather/Crone aspect of the Divine. Use darker-colored candles (already lit) on both sides of the altar as symbolic of their presence. The central candle remains unlit.

Invocation

This invocation can begin in the west, the region of maturity:

WEST
Waters that nourish the land and caress the shores,
saturate our spirits, and this sacred space.
From your wellspring, joy freely pours
to all gathered here in this place.

NORTH
Earth that gives life to beast and flower,
root our spirits, in this circle bound.
From your seeds, magic grows this hour
to bless our elder, as the Wheel turns 'round.

EAST
Air that blows with vital winds,
refresh our spirits, in this sphere of light.
From your breath, magic begins
to bless our elder, now in your sight.

SOUTH
Flames that burn, but never tire,
ignite our spirits, banish the dark.
From your hearth, bring now the fire
to empower our elder, as on this path he/she embarks.

CENTER

The invocation to the center point acts as a prayer:

Spirit, you who were before all things; from whom we were created and pray to return—hold safe the magic in this place, and witness this rite of eldership. Grant unto _____ [name of new elder] the peace of mind with which to continue walking the path of beauty. We thank you for all _____ has given us; for his/her knowledge, insight, and for teachings still yet to be. Hold _____ safe in your loving embrace, and fill him/her with your power anew. So be it.

Meditation and Visualization

Ask the person for whom this ritual is designed what type of meditation he or she might like. For example, perhaps there are things he or she wishes to release before accepting eldership, or other attributes to energize as part of the ritual. These things can be incorporated into the visualization.

The Ritual

The celebrant goes forward and lights his or her candle on the altar. The leader takes him or her by the hand before the altar, saying, *"Power of Creation, Source of All Magic. I present to you now _____, whom we honor as an elder among us. May he/she accept age as a great gift; for one who lives long, learns much, and can bless others with that knowledge. May today represent but one more step along the path of enlightenment."*

The leader begins walking clockwise around the circle, stopping at the elemental points beginning in the east. *"When you were a child, you thought and acted as a child. Today the winds of transformation have brought maturity."*

Moving to the south: *"As you grew up, things always seemed to take forever, but now time slips quickly by. Yet it is not time wasted. The fires of your life have burned brightly, and illuminated much."*

Moving to the west: *"As an adult, responsibilities were many, as* were sorrow and joy. The tears that flow with both have washed your soul anew. Today you begin as one cleansed by time."

Moving to the north: "And now you come full circle, as an elder. The Earth has rooted you in her rich lessons, from which we all hope to grow and learn. Do you freely accept the position we offer you as one so honored among us?"

The celebrant replies, "I do." At this point, if an elder mark has been created (see "Other Activities"), it should be presented. Then people clockwise around the circle present their tokens to the elder, explaining the significance of the item(s).

Other Activities

Some groups find a way to mark their recognized elders at the end of a ritual, often by presenting such items as a belt, medicine shield, pouch, embroidered favor, and the like. This type of emblem can be especially meaningful if everyone in the group can help in its creation, if only by serving coffee during the work session. While people create the token, they should chant, sing sacred songs, and talk about the person for whom it's intended. This will help the token absorb more positive energy.

Closing the Circle

Fill in the blanks in this invocation with the magical or real name of the newly recognized elder among you. I have chosen in this instance to dismiss the quarters *clockwise* as a sign of life's continuance.

SOUTH
Farewell, Guardians of the South and Flame,
may _____'s life, ne'r be the same.

EAST
Farewell, Guardians of the East and Air,
over _____'s life, always take care.

NORTH
Farewell, Guardians of the North and Earth,
grant _____ *a life of mirth.*

WEST
Farewell, Guardians of the West and Rain,
merry we part, and meet again!

No center dismissal is necessary with this, but a final prayer could be added, which is best written and recited by the new elder.

Postritual Food

Try any edible or beverage that grows better with age, such as wine and cheese.

28

Death

Wiccans believe in reincarnation—the idea that upon death a human soul is released from its mortal shell and goes into a kind of hibernation until reborn into a new body. The cycle of reincarnation continues until that soul becomes "enlightened" and can reunite with the Source. So while death is a time of sadness, in Wiccan rituals it is also a time to rejoice—to know that the Wheel is still turning, and that the soul of our loved ones will come back to life just as Earth is reborn in spring. Consider holding Summerland rituals during a new moon, the in-between time before light shines in the night sky once more. The themes of this ritual are emotional healing, the release of the spirit, and reincarnation.

Preparations

From the people attending gather photographs of the deceased, along with white flowers, sweet-smelling incense (which represents the soul), a special candle to represent the deceased on the altar, and a talking stick or wand.

The Altar

The Summerland altar is covered in black, the hue of night, sleep, and dreams. Pictures of the deceased adorn the altar along with white flowers, the color of hope and the eternal spirit. Lily and lotus are good choices. One candle that represents the deceased is already lit, as are any God and Goddess candles.

Invocation

This invocation begins in the west, the traditional resting place of the dead. Fill in the blank with the various names (magical, mundane, and nicknames) of the deceased.

WEST
Guardian of the Land of the Dead, the isle of sleep,
open a gate and guide the one known as _____ to this place safely.
Let his/her spirit flow gently on your waves.

NORTH
Guardian of the Earth Plane, where the living dwell,
allow _____'s spirit to walk among us for a moment.
Tether it with love to this sacred space.

EAST
Guardian of the Air, on which spirits fly,
lift _____ to us, let him/her come on your
warm breath to hear our parting words.

SOUTH
Guardian of the Living Fires, that kindle our soul,
give _____ the energy to share with us this last
moment before his/her spirit returns to your hearth.

CENTER
Dark Lady, Lord of Death, open a gate that _____
might enter this sacred space. Let him/her dance with
us once more; let us hold his/her energy close for
this moment between the worlds.

Meditation and Visualization

Have everyone join hands around the circle.

Visualize this circle, and where you stand right now, as filled with shimmering, silver-white light. It sparkles and dances with life and magic. Feel it all around you, warming the skin; energizing your spirit. Let this power wash away your sadness, your grief, and replace it with peace....

Now, at the western point of the circle, envision the form of _____. This is not his/her earthly form, but spiritual essence. It moves toward us slowly, reaching out hands to join the circle. Open a space at the west so _____ can join us. [Two people in the western quarter drop hands.] *Sense this spirit as it mingles with your own.* [The leader of the meditation now lights the sweet-smelling incense that represents this soul.] *The aroma of _____'s being is among us, celebrating its release and joining in this last circle of magic, the circle of rebirth.*

The Ritual

The leader says, *"We have gathered here to remember one whose spirit will be sorely missed. While we grieve our loss, we rejoice in the freedom and new beginning this represents for _____."* The leader goes to the first person in the western quarter, hands him or her the talking stick or wand, and asks, *"What thoughts will you share about _____?"* This person speaks freely. When he or she finishes, the talking stick is returned to the leader, who takes it to the next person, counterclockwise, and repeats the question. This procedure continues around the circle until all gathered have spoken.

Other Activities

A memory circle can be a very healing experience. For this, all participants sit in the sacred space and talk about their memories openly. This is far less structured than the talking stick approach, but other people should still provide whatever emotional support seems appropriate to the moment.

Also, consider adding a prayer for souls who have not moved from the Earth plane—that they might find peace.

Closing the Circle

Instead of a standard dismissal, this rite ends by saying goodbye and a prayer:

"*Now dear friend, we say goodbye. Let your spirit fly free from this mortal realm. Have no fear; we will be well. Join your fellows in Summerland; let your spirit rest and refresh. And when the time comes, return to this world in a new, healthy body that will allow your quest for union with the One to continue.*"

The leader blows out the individual's candle. "*Great Lord and Lady, we commit _____ into your gentle care. Watch well his/her soul until it is reborn. Powers of the Four Winds, as you depart from this place, help those of us here who grieve to heal and hope and remember. The Wheel has turned once more, and will yet again. So let it be.*"

Postritual Foods

As a way of remembering your loved one, prepare foods that he or she enjoyed in life. Leave a little of this aside on a special plate so that the deceased's spirit can partake of it metaphorically. Afterward, give it to the creatures of Nature to enjoy.

Afterword

I by no means consider myself an undisputed authority on the numerous forms of Wicca and its associated rituals. The rituals in this book, therefore, reflect only a small portion of what can be a very complex faith. Consequently, I recommend that individuals new to Wicca and its precepts read *Drawing Down the Moon* by Margot Adler to get a better feel for the diversity of traditions that Wicca offers. Also browse texts, such as *The History of Magic* by Richard Cavendish. This will give you a good idea of where magic has been, and where it may be going in the future.

My path in the Craft is very eclectic, mingling numerous traditions and world faiths into a personally pleasing blend. This road is not necessarily one that everyone can, or should, walk. Give yourself the opportunity to review as many Wiccan groups as possible before committing yourself to one specific route. And even once you walk that path, don't set your footprints in concrete. Let life and its lessons guide your way, so that Wicca and its special energy grow with you, with those people who touch your life, and with the world.

Blessed be.

Index